THE BIBLE OF COMMON ITALIAN PHRASES FOR EVERYDAY USE [3 BOOKS IN 1]

2000+ Phrases with Must-Know
Local Slang and the Funniest
Distinctive Dialectal Sayings To
Immerse Yourself in Italian Culture

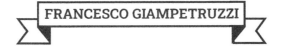
FRANCESCO GIAMPETRUZZI

CONTENTS

EVERYDAY ITALIAN PHRASES

ITALIAN SLANG

ITALIAN TRADITIONS, ETIQUETTE AND CURIOSITIES

ABOUT FRANCESCO

Hello to you who have this book in your hands and are probably planning to come and visit my beloved Italy!

Before I leave you to read, I wanted to introduce myself: my name is Francesco Giampetruzzi, known to my friends as "Petrù", I live in Puglia, in the southern part of Italy, and I am 26 years old.

I am a farmer with over 7000 trees, including olive, almond, and many other types of fruits, but I also have a passion for traveling and welcoming tourists from all over the world. In particular, Finland kidnapped my heart and continues to kidnap it whenever I return.

But as much as I adore Finland, my love for the land where I was born remains indescribable. I live in the center of many of Puglia's beauties, such as Polignano a Mare, Alberobello, Castellana Grotte, Matera, Monopoli, Bari, Ostuni, Locorotondo, and many other towns full of history, culture, and traditions that, besides me, tourists love!

In addition, the food we produce here has something extraordinary: genuine, high-quality, farm-to-table flavors and ingredients with exceptional properties conferred by the land, sea, and wind of this region, which I would very much like you to taste.

I also love to travel to all the other beautiful Italian cities that have so much to offer, such as natural landscapes, beautiful art cities, museums, tourist attractions, and so much more!

But let's go back to the book you are about to read.

Now that you are planning to visit Italy, I must warn you that you are getting into a lot of trouble: it will not be easy at all to choose what to visit from the hundreds of wonderful places Italy has to offer!

Therefore, to enable you to talk to Italians by saying phrases that will get you into the heart of Italian culture, I have made this simple phrasebook!

I love welcoming tourists from all over the world, so if you ever need help visiting Puglia, I suggest you check out my site and my Instagram.

You may decide to let an authentic Apulian guide you to discover the most beautiful places in my country!

I wish you a fantastic read, with the hope of seeing you here soon!

A hug,

Francesco

HAVE A GOOD
TRAVEL!

EVERYDAY ITALIAN PHRASES

INTRODUCTION: HOW TO READ ITALIAN

The first stage for a native speaker of English or American English is to learn how to read and pronounce the Italian alphabet.

The English and Italian alphabets are identical, and they consist of the letters A through Z.

The letters J, K, W, X, Y are not found in words of Italian origin but are used in foreign words embedded in the language.

Each letter has a specific and, for the most part, constant pronunciation.

Here is a brief summary of the pronunciations:

- A —> The "A" in "Father"
- B —> The "B" in "Boy"
- C —> If in front of "E" or "I", is like "CH" in "Cheese" otherwise it is like 'k' in "king"
- D —> 'D' in "dog"
- E —> It can sound like the "E" in "Pen" or like "Ay" in "Day"
- F —> 'F' in "fish"

- G: in front of 'E' or 'I', it is similar to 'G' in "giant"; otherwise it is like 'g' in "go"
- H: always silent, but changes pronunciation of 'c' and 'g' when placed after
- I: —> 'ee' in "see"
- L: —> 'l' in "love"
- M —> 'm' in "mom"
- N: —> 'n' in "no"
- O: two possible sounds, similar to 'o' in "pot" or like 'o' in "bone"
- P —> 'p' in "pen"
- Q: always followed by 'u' and pronounced like 'q' in "queen"
- R: rolled, louder than 'r' in "right"
- S: between two vowels is like 'z' in "haze," otherwise like 's' in "sun"
- T —> 't' in "top"
- U: —> 'oo' in "too"
- V —> 'v' in "vine"
- Z: two possible sounds, like 'ts' in "bits" or like 'dz'

Remember that in Italian every word is pronounced exactly as it is spelled. This makes learning pronunciation much easier than in other languages. Every letter in a word is pronounced; there are no silent letters, except for the h, which is not pronounced but changes the sound of the word.

In addition, Italian is a "phonetic" language, which means that most words are pronounced as they are written. Vowels, in particular, almost always keep the same sound, which is a very important aspect of Italian pronunciation.

Also pay attention to double consonants (such as 'tt', 'll', 'rr', etc.), these need to be pronounced longer. For example, the word 'palla' (meaning 'ball') has two 'l's that must be pronounced distinctly.

The Italian language is melodious and each word seems to flow into the next. Practice pronunciation by reading aloud, listening to the language spoken by native speakers and, if possible, participate in conversations in Italian.

Remember, learning a new language is a journey, not a destination. Take your time, enjoy the process, and soon you will find yourself speaking and under-standing Italian with a new confidence and ease. Welcome to the wonderful world of the Italian language!

THE CHARM OF THE ITALIAN LANGUAGE

There's an undeniable allure to the Italian language that captivates the heart and mind. It's a language of warmth, full of expressive vowels and eloquent gestures that mirror the country's vibrant landscapes and the soul of its people.

Italian is rooted in the birthplace of the Renaissance, a period that drastically changed the world's approach to art, science, music, and thought. This history is embedded within each spoken word, creating a palpable connection to a cultural past that influenced the course of human development.

Moreover, Italian words often feel like more than mere combinations of letters.

They carry an emotional weight, adding depth and passion to everyday conversation. The rolling "r"s, the soft "l"s, the melodic intonations – each element weaves a unique auditory experience that is as pleasurable to hear as it is to speak.

Whether you're expressing love, ordering food, or discussing art, speaking Italian imbues an enchanting quality to communication, transforming ordinary conversations into melodic symphonies of human connection. This is the charm of the Italian language.

THE IMPORTANCE OF KNOWING ITALIAN

Knowing Italian opens a multitude of doors, both personally and professionally.

As the third most spoken language in Europe and one of the EU's official languages, Italian carries considerable weight in cross-cultural exchanges.

It is the language of culture, art, gastronomy, fashion, and design, which makes it an essential tool for those involved in these industries.

On a personal level, learning Italian enables a richer, deeper understanding of Italy's cultural heritage.

With a command of the language, one can directly access Italy's vast literary treasures, appreciate its rich cinematic history, and engage in the country's renowned gastronomic culture with a deeper understanding.

Additionally, for travelers, knowing Italian significantly enhances the experience of visiting Italy.You'll be able to engage with the locals on a deeper level, learn more about the culture, and go around with more assurance if you know the language.Learning a new language also has been shown to improve mental faculties.It enhances mental agility, improves memory, and even delays the onset of dementia.

Thus, knowing Italian is not just a cultural asset but also a contribution to one's cognitive health.

In a globalized world, language proficiency is no longer a luxury but a necessity.

And learning Italian, with its rich cultural heritage and global relevance, is indeed a valuable pursuit.

STRUCTURE OF THE BOOK AND HOW TO USE IT

This book, "Italian 24/7: Master the Language for Every Moment of the Day", is designed to be your constant companion in your journey to master Italian.

The 20 chapters of this book cover a wide range of topics, from the sentences to say in the morning to the ones to tell when you spend your night, and everything in between.

In each chapter you can find numerous examples of phrases, expressions, and conversations that are typically used in Italian situations.

For ease of use, each phrase or expression is presented first in Italian, then in English, and finally phonetically.

This book will give you a better idea of what the most common Italian phrases mean, and how to pronunce them correctly to be understood by everyone in Italy!

You are free to read the chapters in whatever order you like, or to skip forward to those that particularly grab your attention.

It can be used as a quick reference or as a resource for further in-depth research.

Remember, the most important part of language learning is practice.

Don't just read the phrases and conversations - speak them out loud, write them down, use them in your daily life.You'll start sounding more and more like a native Italian speaker the more time you spend immersed in the language.

Buona fortuna!

(Good luck!)

THE COLORS

MAIN COLORS

1. "Black" - "Nero" [NEH-ro]
2. "White" - "Bianco" [BYAHN-koh]
3. "Red" - "Rosso" [ROH-soh]
4. "Blue" - "Blu" [bloo]
5. "Yellow" - "Giallo" [JAH-loh]
6. "Green" - "Verde" [VEHR-deh]
7. "Purple" - "Viola" [VYOH-lah]
8. "Orange" - "Arancione" [ah-ran-CHOH-neh]
9. "Pink" - "Rosa" [ROH-sah]
10. "Brown" - "Marrone" [mah-ROH-neh]
11. "Grey" - "Grigio" [GREE-joh]
12. "Gold" - "Oro" [OH-roh]
13. "Silver" - "Argento" [ar-GEN-toh]

14. "Cyan" - "Ciano" [CHEE-ah-noh]
15. "Magenta" - "Magenta" [mah-JEN-tah]
16. "Turquoise" - "Turchese" [toor-KEH-zeh]
17. "Lime" - "Lime" [lahym]
18. "Indigo" - "Indaco" [in-DAH-koh]
19. "Teal" - "Verde acqua" [VEHR-deh AH-kwah]
20. "Maroon" - "Granata" [grah-NAH-tah]

SENTENCES WITH COLORS

1. "The black cat crossed the street." - "Il gatto nero ha attraversato la strada." [eel GAHT-toh NEH-roh ah ah-tra-ver-SA-toh lah STAH-dah]"She bought a red dress." - "Lei ha comprato un vestito rosso." [leh-ee ah kohm-PRAH-toh oon veh-STEET-toh ROH-soh]
2. "The sky is blue." - "Il cielo è blu." [eel CHYEH-loh eh bloo]
3. "Yellow sunflowers make me happy." - "I girasoli gialli mi rendono felice." [ee jee-rah-SOH-lee JAH-lee mee REN-doh-noh feh-LEE-cheh]
4. "The green grass is damp." - "L'erba verde è umida." [LEHR-bah VEHR-deh eh oo-MEE-dah]
5. "She has purple eyes." - "Lei ha gli occhi viola." [leh-ee ah llee OHK-kee VYOH-lah]
6. "I want an orange car." - "Voglio una macchina arancione." [VOHL-yoh oo-nah mahk-KEE-nah ah-ran-CHOH-neh]
7. "His cheeks turned pink." - "Le sue guance sono diventate rosa." [leh soo-eh GWAN-cheh SOH-noh dee-ven-TAH-teh ROH-sah]
8. "The old man's hair is grey." - "I capelli del vecchio sono grigi." [ee ka-PELL-ee del VECK-yoh SOH-noh GREE-jee]
9. "He gave her a gold necklace." - "Le ha dato una collana d'oro." [leh ah DAH-toh oo-nah koh-LAH-nah DOH-ro]
10. "Cyan is a refreshing and vibrant color." - "Il ciano è un colore rinfrescante e vibrante." [Eel chee-AH-no eh oon KO-loh-reh reen-FREH-scan-teh e vee-BRAN-teh]
11. "Magenta is a rich and intense color." - "Il magenta è un colore ricco e intenso." [Eel ma-JEN-ta eh oon KO-loh-reh REEK-ko e een-TEN-so]
12. "Turquoise is a calming and soothing color." - "Il turchese è un colore calmo e rilassante." [Eel toor-KEH-zeh eh oon KO-loh-reh KAL-mo e ree-lahs-SAN-teh]
13. "Lime is a vibrant and zesty color." - "Il lime è un colore vivace e frizzante." [Eel LEE-meh eh oon KO-loh-reh vee-VAH-cheh e freet-ZAHN-teh]
14. "Indigo is a deep and mysterious color." - "L'indaco è un colore profondo e misterioso." [LEEN-dah-koh eh oon KO-loh-reh pro-FON-do e mee-steh-ree-OH-so]
15. "Teal is a cool and soothing color." - "Il turchese scuro è un colore fresco e rilassante." [Eel toor-KEH-zeh SKOO-roh eh oon KO-loh-reh FREH-skoh e ree-lahs-SAN-teh]

8

16. "Maroon is a rich and elegant color." - "Il marrone è un colore ricco ed elegante." [Eel mar-ROH-neh eh oon KO-loh-reh REEK-ko ed eh-leh-GAN-teh]

NUMBERS

NUMBERS FROM 1 TO 100

1. "One" - "Uno" - [OO-no]
2. "Two" - "Due" - [DOO-eh]
3. "Three" - "Tre" - [TREH]
4. "Four" - "Quattro" - [KWAH-tro]
5. "Five" - "Cinque" - [CHEEN-kweh]
6. "Six" - "Sei" - [SEH-ee]
7. "Seven" - "Sette" - [SEHT-teh]
8. "Eight" - "Otto" - [OH-to]
9. "Nine" - "Nove" - [NOH-veh]
10. "Ten" - "Dieci" - [DYEH-chee]
11. "Eleven" - "Undici" - [oon-DEE-chee]
12. "Twelve" - "Dodici" - [doh-DEE-chee]
13. "Thirteen" - "Tredici" - [treh-DEE-chee]
14. "Fourteen" - "Quattordici" - [kwaht-tor-DEE-chee]

15. "Fifteen" - "Quindici" - [kween-DEE-chee]
16. "Sixteen" - "Sedici" - [seh-DEE-chee]
17. "Seventeen" - "Diciassette" - [dee-chahs-SEH-teh]
18. "Eighteen" - "Diciotto" - [dee-CHOH-toh]
19. "Nineteen" - "Diciannove" - [dee-chan-NOH-veh]
20. "Twenty" - "Venti" - [VEN-tee]
21. "Twenty-one" - "Ventuno" - [ven-TOO-noh]
22. "Twenty-two" - "Ventidue" - [ven-tee-DOO-eh]
23. "Twenty-three" - "Ventitré" - [ven-tee-TREH]
24. "Twenty-four" - "Ventiquattro" - [ven-tee-KWAT-troh]
25. "Twenty-five" - "Venticinque" - [ven-tee-CHEEN-kweh]
26. "Twenty-six" - "Ventisei" - [ven-tee-SEH-ee]
27. "Twenty-seven" - "Ventisette" - [ven-tee-SEH-teh]
28. "Twenty-eight" - "Ventotto" - [ven-TOH-toh]
29. "Twenty-nine" - "Ventinove" - [ven-tee-NOH-veh]
30. "Thirty" - "Trenta" - [TREN-tah]
31. "Thirty-one" - "Trentuno" - [tren-TOO-noh]
32. "Thirty-two" - "Trentadue" - [tren-ta-DOO-eh]
33. "Thirty-three" - "Trentatré" - [tren-ta-TREH]
34. "Thirty-four" - "Trentaquattro" - [tren-ta-KWAT-troh]
35. "Thirty-five" - "Trentacinque" - [tren-ta-CHEEN-kweh]
36. "Thirty-six" - "Trentasei" - [tren-ta-SEH-ee]
37. "Thirty-seven" - "Trentasette" - [tren-ta-SEH-teh]
38. "Thirty-eight" - "Trentotto" - [tren-TOH-toh]
39. "Thirty-nine" - "Trentanove" - [tren-ta-NOH-veh]
40. "Forty" - "Quaranta" - [kwa-RAN-tah]
41. "Forty-one" - "Quarantuno" - [kwa-ran-TOO-noh]
42. "Forty-two" - "Quarantadue" - [kwa-ran-ta-DOO-eh]
43. "Forty-three" - "Quarantatré" - [kwa-ran-ta-TREH]
44. "Forty-four" - "Quarantaquattro" - [kwa-ran-ta-KWAT-troh]
45. "Forty-five" - "Quarantacinque" - [kwa-ran-ta-CHEEN-kweh]
46. "Forty-six" - "Quarantasei" - [kwa-ran-ta-SEH-ee]
47. "Forty-seven" - "Quarantasette" - [kwa-ran-ta-SEH-teh]
48. "Forty-eight" - "Quarantotto" - [kwa-ran-TOH-toh]
49. "Forty-nine" - "Quarantanove" - [kwa-ran-ta-NOH-veh]
50. "Fifty" - "Cinquanta" - [cheen-KWAN-tah]
51. "Fifty-one" - "Cinquantuno" - [cheen-kwan-TOO-noh]
52. "Fifty-two" - "Cinquantadue" - [cheen-kwan-ta-DOO-eh]
53. "Fifty-three" - "Cinquantatré" - [cheen-kwan-ta-TREH]
54. "Fifty-four" - "Cinquantaquattro" - [cheen-kwan-ta-KWAT-troh]
55. "Fifty-five" - "Cinquantacinque" - [cheen-kwan-ta-CHEEN-kweh]
56. "Fifty-six" - "Cinquantasei" - [cheen-kwan-ta-SEH-ee]
57. "Fifty-seven" - "Cinquantasette" - [cheen-kwan-ta-SEH-teh]
58. "Fifty-eight" - "Cinquantotto" - [cheen-kwan-TOH-toh]
59. "Fifty-nine" - "Cinquantanove" - [cheen-kwan-ta-NOH-veh]
60. "Sixty" - "Sessanta" - [seh-SAN-tah]

61. "Sixty-one" - "Sessantuno" - [seh-san-TOO-noh]
62. "Sixty-two" - "Sessantadue" - [seh-san-ta-DOO-eh]
63. "Sixty-three" - "Sessantatré" - [seh-san-ta-TREH]
64. "Sixty-four" - "Sessantaquattro" - [seh-san-ta-KWAT-troh]
65. "Sixty-five" - "Sessantacinque" - [seh-san-ta-CHEEN-kweh]
66. "Sixty-six" - "Sessantasei" - [seh-san-ta-SEH-ee]
67. "Sixty-seven" - "Sessantasette" - [seh-san-ta-SEH-teh]
68. "Sixty-eight" - "Sessantotto" - [seh-san-TOH-toh]
69. "Sixty-nine" - "Sessantanove" - [seh-san-ta-NOH-veh]
70. "Seventy" - "Settanta" - [seh-TAN-tah]
71. "Seventy-one" - "Settantuno" - [seh-tan-TOO-noh]
72. "Seventy-two" - "Settantadue" - [seh-tan-ta-DOO-eh]
73. "Seventy-three" - "Settantatré" - [seh-tan-ta-TREH]
74. "Seventy-four" - "Settantaquattro" - [seh-tan-ta-KWAT-troh]
75. "Seventy-five" - "Settantacinque" - [seh-tan-ta-CHEEN-kweh]
76. "Seventy-six" - "Settantasei" - [seh-tan-ta-SEH-ee]
77. "Seventy-seven" - "Settantasette" - [seh-tan-ta-SEH-teh]
78. "Seventy-eight" - "Settantotto" - [seh-tan-TOH-toh]
79. "Seventy-nine" - "Settantanove" - [seh-tan-ta-NOH-veh]
80. "Eighty" - "Ottanta" - [oh-TAN-tah]
81. "Eighty-one" - "Ottantuno" - [oh-tan-TOO-noh]
82. "Eighty-two" - "Ottantadue" - [oh-tan-ta-DOO-eh]
83. "Eighty-three" - "Ottantatré" - [oh-tan-ta-TREH]
84. "Eighty-four" - "Ottantaquattro" - [oh-tan-ta-KWAT-troh]
85. "Eighty-five" - "Ottantacinque" - [oh-tan-ta-CHEEN-kweh]
86. "Eighty-six" - "Ottantasei" - [oh-tan-ta-SEH-ee]
87. "Eighty-seven" - "Ottantasette" - [oh-tan-ta-SEH-teh]
88. "Eighty-eight" - "Ottantotto" - [oh-tan-TOH-toh]
89. "Eighty-nine" - "Ottantanove" - [oh-tan-ta-NOH-veh]
90. "Ninety" - "Novanta" - [no-VAN-tah]
91. "Ninety-one" - "Novantuno" - [no-van-TOO-noh]
92. "Ninety-two" - "Novantadue" - [no-van-ta-DOO-eh]
93. "Ninety-three" - "Novantatré" - [no-van-ta-TREH]
94. "Ninety-four" - "Novantaquattro" - [no-van-ta-KWAT-troh]
95. "Ninety-five" - "Novantacinque" - [no-van-ta-CHEEN-kweh]
96. "Ninety-six" - "Novantasei" - [no-van-ta-SEH-ee]
97. "Ninety-seven" - "Novantasette" - [no-van-ta-SEH-teh]
98. "Ninety-eight" - "Novantotto" - [no-van-TOH-toh]
99. "Ninety-nine" - "Novantanove" - [no-van-ta-NOH-veh]
100. "One hundred" - "Cento" - [CHEN-toh]

Numbers such as 200, 300, 400 etc. are easy to pronounce, just add the number before 100, like this:

1. "Two hundred" - "Duecento" - [doo-eh-CHEN-toh]
2. "Three hundred" - "Trecento" - [treh-CHEN-toh]
3. "Four hundred" - "Quattrocento" - [kwa-troh-CHEN-toh]
4. "Five hundred" - "Cinquecento" - [cheen-kweh-CHEN-toh]
5. "Six hundred" - "Seicento" - [seh-ee-CHEN-toh]
6. "Seven hundred" - "Settecento" - [seh-teh-CHEN-toh]
7. "Eight hundred" - "Ottocento" - [ot-toh-CHEN-toh]
8. "Nine hundred" - "Novecento" - [no-veh-CHEN-toh]

This is how to read numbers with three zeros:

1. "One thousand" - "Mille" - [MEE-leh]
2. "Two thousand" - "Duemila" - [dweh-MEE-lah]
3. "Three thousand" - "Tremila" - [treh-MEE-lah]
4. "Four thousand" - "Quattromila" - [kwah-troh-MEE-lah]
5. "Five thousand" - "Cinquemila" - [cheen-kweh-MEE-lah]
6. "Six thousand" - "Seimila" - [seh-ee-MEE-lah]
7. "Seven thousand" - "Settemila" - [seh-teh-MEE-lah]
8. "Eight thousand" - "Ottomila" - [ot-toh-MEE-lah]
9. "Nine thousand" - "Novemila" - [no-veh-MEE-lah]

And finally:

1. 10,000. "Ten thousand" - "Diecimila" - [dee-eh-CHEE-mee-lah]
2. 100,000. "One hundred thousand" - "Cento-mila" - [CHEN-toh-MEE-lah]
3. 1,000,000. "One million" - "Un milione" - [oon mee-lee-OH-neh]
4. 1,000,000,000. "One billion" - "Un miliardo" - [oon mee-lee-AHR-doh]

Note: The term "billion" in Italian refers to 1,000,000,000 (one billion in the long scale). In the short scale, which is more commonly used, "billion" refers to 1,000,000,000,000 (one trillion).

SENTENCES WITH NUMBERS

1. "I bought 3 new books today." - "Ho comprato 3 libri nuovi oggi." [Oh kohm-PRYAH-toh treh LEE-bree NOO-vee OHG-ghee]
2. "I went to dinner with 5 friends last night." - "Sono andato a cena con 5 amici ieri sera." [SOH-noh ahn-DAH-toh ah CHEH-nah kohn KWEHN-troh ah-MEE-tchee YE-eh-ree SEH-rah]

3. "My favorite cake is number 7, chocolate-flavored." - "La mia torta preferita è la numero 7, al cioccolato." [Lah MEE-ah TOR-tah preh-feh-REE-tah eh lah NOO-meh-roh SET-teh, ahl chohk-oh-LAH-toh]
4. "I traveled to 10 different countries during the holidays." - "Ho viaggiato in 10 paesi diversi durante le vacanze." [Oh vee-AH-tchee-ah-toh een DEH-chee pah-EH-zee dee-VEHR-see DOO-RAHN-teh leh vah-KAHN-tseh]
5. "My favorite soccer team won 4-0." - "La mia squadra di calcio preferita ha vinto per 4-0." [Lah MEE-ah SKWOH-drah dee KAL-choh preh-feh-REE-tah ah VEEN-toh pehr KWAH-troh OH]
6. "I received an important phone call at 9 in the morning." - "Ho ricevuto una telefonata importante alle 9 di mattina." [Oh ree-cheh-VOO-toh OO-nah te-leh-foh-NAH-tah eem-por-TAHN-teh AHL-leh NOH-veh dee maht-TEE-nah]
7. "I spent 6 hours reading my favorite book." - "Ho trascorso 6 ore a leggere il mio libro preferito." [Oh trah-SKOR-soh SEH-ee OR-eh ah leh-GEH-reh eel MEE-oh LEE-broh preh-feh-REE-toh]
8. "I cooked a delicious recipe that required 2 cups of sugar." - "Ho cucinato una ricetta deliziosa che richiedeva 2 tazze di zucchero." [Oh koo-chee-NAH-toh OO-nah ree-CHEHT-tah deh-lee-ZYOH-sah keh ree-kyeh-DEH-vah DOO TAT-tseh dee tsook-KEH-roh]
9. "I went to the cinema to see the 12th film of the saga." - "Sono stato al cinema per vedere il film numero 12 della saga." [SOH-noh STAH-toh ahl CHEE-nem-ah pehr veh-DEH-reh eel FEELM NOO-meh-roh DOH-dee-chee-ehs dee-LAH SAH-gah]
10. "I enjoy taking 2-hour walks in the park every day." - "Mi piace fare passeggiate di 2 ore nel parco ogni giorno." [Mee PYAH-cheh FAH-reh pahs-seh-JAH-teh dee DOO OR-eh nehl PAHR-koh OH-nee JOHR-noh]

TIME AND DATE

Knowing how to ask for directions is essential for arranging appointments, planning sightseeing, finding your way around a new city, and more when you are abroad.

In this chapter will see how to ask and tell the time, express dates, days of the week, and months of the year, and use a variety of useful expressions for asking and giving directions.

Get ready to explore how time and space are expressed in the beautiful Italian language!

COMMON WORDS RELATED TO TIME

1. "Hour" - "Ora" - [OH-rah]
2. "Minute" - "Minuto" - [mee-NOO-toh]
3. "Second" - "Secondo" - [se-KON-doh]
4. "Time" - "Tempo" - [TEM-poh]
5. "Clock" - "Orologio" - [o-ROH-loh-joh]

6. "Morning" - "Mattina" - [mah-TEE-nah]
7. "Afternoon" - "Pomeriggio" - [poh-meh-REE-joh]
8. "Evening" - "Sera" - [SEH-rah]
9. "Night" - "Notte" - [NOH-teh]
10. "Midnight" - "Mezzanotte" - [mehd-zah-NOH-teh]
11. "Noon" - "Mezzogiorno" - [mehd-zoh-JOHR-noh]
12. "Early" - "Presto" - [PREH-stoh]
13. "Late" - "Tardi" - [TAHR-dee]
14. "Schedule" - "Orario" - [oh-RAH-ree-oh]
15. "Day" - "Giorno" - [JOHR-noh]
16. "Week" - "Settimana" - [seht-tee-MAH-nah]
17. "Month" - "Mese" - [MEH-seh]
18. "Year" - "Anno" - [AHN-noh]
19. "Calendar" - "Calendario" - [kah-lehn-DAH-ree-oh]
20. "Daylight Saving Time" - "Ora Legale" - [OH-rah leh-GAH-leh]

USEFUL PHRASES ABOUT TIME

1. "What time is it?" - "Che ora è?" [KEH OH-rah eh]
2. "It's three o'clock." - "Sono le tre." [SOH-noh leh TREH]
3. "Can we meet in the afternoon?" - "Possiamo incontrarci nel pomeriggio?" [POH-see-ah-moh in-kon-trar-chee nel poh-meh-REE-joh]
4. "I will arrive early in the morning." - "Arriverò di mattina presto." [ar-ri-VEH-roh dee mah-TEE-nah PREH-stoh]
5. "The shop closes late at night." - "Il negozio chiude tardi la notte." [eel neh-GOH-tsee-oh KEE-oo-deh TAHR-dee lah NOH-teh]
6. "See you tomorrow." - "Ci vediamo domani." [chee veh-DYAH-moh doh-MAH-nee]
7. "The meeting is scheduled for next week." - "La riunione è programmata per la prossima settimana." [lah ree-OO-nee-oh-neh eh proh-GRAM-mah-tah pehr lah PROHS-see-mah seh-tee-MAH-nah]
8. "It's half past two." - "Sono le due e mezza." [SOH-noh leh DOO-eh eh MEHD-za]
9. "I will see you in an hour." - "Ci vediamo in un'ora." [chee veh-DYAH-moh in oon-OH-rah]
10. "The movie starts at seven o'clock." - "Il film inizia alle sette." [eel film in-EE-tsee-ah AHL-leh SEHT-teh]
11. "The bus arrives at quarter past six." - "L'autobus arriva alle sei e un quarto." [l'ow-toh-BOOS ah-REE-vah AHL-leh SEH-ee eh oon KWAR-toh]
12. "The concert finishes at midnight." - "Il concerto finisce a mezzanotte." [eel kon-CHEHR-toh fee-NEE-sheh ah mehd-zah-NOH-teh]
13. "I usually go to bed late." - "Di solito vado a letto tardi." [dee SOH-lee-toh VAH-doh ah LET-toh TAHR-dee]

16

14. "The museum opens at nine in the morning." - "Il museo apre alle nove del mattino." [eel MOO-seh-oh AH-preh AHL-leh NOH-veh del mah-TEE-noh]
15. "We have a reservation for eight o'clock." - "Abbiamo una prenotazione per le otto." [ah-BYAH-moh OOH-nah preh-noh-tah-TSYOH-neh pehr leh OHT-toh]
16. "Tomorrow's meeting has been postponed to the afternoon." - "La riunione di domani è stata rimandata al pomeriggio." [lah ree-OO-nee-oh-neh dee doh-MAH-nee eh STAH-tah ree-man-DAH-tah ahl poh-meh-REE-joh]
17. "Lunch is at noon." - "Il pranzo è a mezzogiorno." [eel PRAHN-tsoh eh ah mehd-zoh-JOHR-noh]
18. "The library closes in half an hour." - "La biblioteca chiude tra mezz'ora." [lah bee-blee-oh-TEH-kah KEE-oo-deh trah MEHDZ-oh-rah]
19. "I have a break at ten o'clock." - "Ho una pausa alle dieci." [oh OOH-nah PAH-wzah AHL-leh DYEH-chee]
20. "See you next week." - "Ci vediamo la prossima settimana." [chee veh-DYAH-moh lah PROHS-see-mah seh-tee-MAH-nah]

3 SIMPLE STEPS TO ALWAYS CARRY THIS BOOK WITH YOU IN YOUR POCKET:

1) SCAN THIS QR WITH YOUR CAMERA

2) DOWNLOAD THE FREE PDF VERSION

3) READ IT FROM YOUR SMARTPHONE WHILE TRAVELING IN ITALY!

A FREE BOOK
FOR YOU!

✓ **PUGLIA'S 5 MUST-VISIT LOCATIONS**
✓ **MORE THAN 50 AMAZING BEACHES**
✓ **A NATIVE'S ADVICE ON PUGLIA'S TASTIEST**
✓ **200+ BEAUTIFUL FULL-COLOR PHOTOS TO HELP YOU**
EASILY CHOOSE ACTIVITIES TO INCLUDE IN YOUR TRIP

SCAN THIS QR AND
DOWNLOAD NOW
YOUR FREE BONUS!

START THE DAY

Buongiorno! As the sun rises over the picturesque landscapes of Italy, a new day of adventure and learning begins. Our first chapter, "Good Morning Italy: Phrases to Start the Day," aims to prepare you for every early morning scenario you might encounter. Whether you're ordering your first cappuccino of the day at a bustling Italian café, exchanging pleasantries with your B&B host, or navigating your way to a historical landmark, the right phrases and expressions can make all the difference. This chapter will equip you with a range of essential phrases to start your day on the right foot and experience Italian mornings like a local. Ready to greet the day, Italian style? Cominciamo!

COMMON MORNING WORDS

1. "Morning" - "Mattina" - [mah-TEE-nah]
2. "Breakfast" - "Colazione" - [koh-lah-TSYOH-neh]
3. "Sunrise" - "Alba" - [AHL-bah]
4. "Early" - "Presto" - [PREH-stoh]

5. "Wake up" - "Svegliarsi" - [sveh-lyahr-SEE]
6. "Coffee" - "Caffè" - [kah-FEH]
7. "Toast" - "Pane tostato" - [PAH-neh toh-STAH-toh]
8. "Alarm" - "Sveglia" - [sveh-LYAH]
9. "Shower" - "Doccia" - [DOH-cha]
10. "Dawn" - "Aurora" - [ow-ROH-rah]
11. "Jogging" - "Jogging" - [JOG-ging]
12. "Yawning" - "Sbadigliare" - [zba-deel-YAH-reh]
13. "Stretching" - "Stiracchiarsi" - [stee-rahk-kyahr-SEE]
14. "Morning routine" - "Routine mattutina" - [roo-TEEN-e mah-too-TEE-nah]
15. "Newspaper" - "Giornale" - [johr-NAH-leh]
16. "Cereal" - "Cereali" - [cheh-reh-AH-lee]
17. "Toothbrush" - "Spazzolino" - [spat-tso-LEE-noh]
18. "Toothpaste" - "Dentifricio" - [den-tee-FREE-choh]
19. "Rush hour" - "Ora di punta" - [OH-rah dee POON-tah]
20. "Morning rush" - "Fretta mattutina" - [FREH-tah mah-too-TEE-nah]

MORNING GREETINGS

1. "Good morning!" - "Buongiorno!" [bwohn-JOHR-noh]
2. "Good morning, how are you?" - "Buon giorno, come sta?" [bwohn JOHR-noh, KOH-meh stah]
3. "Hi, have a good day!" - "Ciao, buona giornata!" - [CHOW, bwoh-nah johr-NAH-tah]
4. "Hello, how is your morning going?" - "Salve, come va la mattina?" [SAL-veh, KOH-meh vah lah mah-TEE-nah]
5. "I hope you're having a beautiful day." - "Spero che tu stia passando una bella giornata." [SPEH-roh keh too STYAH pass-AHN-doh OO-nah BEHL-lah johr-NAH-tah]
6. "Have a good awakening!" - "Buon risveglio!" [bwohn ris-veh-GLYOH]
7. "Hope you're having a fantastic day!" - "Spero che tu stia trascorrendo una giornata fantastica!" - [SPEH-roh keh too STYAH trah-skor-REN-doh OO-nah johr-NAH-tah fahn-TAH-stee-kah]
8. "Wishing you a productive and successful day!" - "Ti auguro una giornata produttiva e piena di successi!" - [TEE ow-GOO-roo OO-nah johr-NAH-tah proh-DUT-tee-vah eh PYEH-nah dee soo-CHES-see]
9. "Make the most of your day and enjoy every moment!" - "Approfitta al massimo della tua giornata e goditi ogni istante!" - [ah-proh-FEET-tah al MAHS-see-moh DEL-lah TOO-ah johr-NAH-tah eh goh-DEE-tee OH-nee een-STAHN-teh]
10. "May your day be filled with love and happiness!" - "Che la tua giornata sia piena di amore e felicità!" - [keh lah TOO-ah johr-NAH-tah SEE-ah PYEH-nah dee ah-MOH-reh eh feh-lee-CHEE-tah]
11. "How was your night?" - "Come è andata la notte?" - [KOH-meh eh AHN-dah-tah lah NOH-teh]

23

12. "Good morning, did you sleep well?" - "Buon giorno, hai dormito bene?"
    - [BWOHN JOHR-no, AI dor-MEE-toh BEH-neh]
13. "It's a beautiful day!" - "È una bella giornata!" - [EH OO-nah BEHL-lah
    johr-NAH-tah]
14. "Good awakening! May you have a day full of energy." - "Buon risveglio!
    Che tu possa avere una giornata piena di energia." - [BWOHN ris-veh-
    GLYOH! KEH too POH-ssah ah-VEH-reh OO-nah johr-NAH-tah
    PYEH-nah dee eh-NEHR-gee-ah]
15. "What's your plan for today?" - "Che programma hai per oggi?" - [KEH
    pro-GRAM-mah AI pehr OH-jee]
16. "Good morning, ready for a new adventure?" - "Buon giorno, pronti per
    una nuova avventura?" - [BWOHN JOHR-no, PROHN-tee pehr OO-
    nah NOO-vah av-vehn-TOO-rah]
17. "May you enjoy every moment of this day." - "Che tu possa goderti ogni
    istante di questa giornata." - [KEH too POH-ssah goh-DEHR-tee OH-
    nee ees-TAHN-teh dee KWEH-stah johr-NAH-tah]
18. "Good morning, have you had your coffee yet?" - "Buon giorno, hai già
    preso il tuo caffè?" - [BWOHN JOHR-no, AI JAH preh-ZOH eel TOO-
    oh KA-feh]
19. "May you start the day with a smile." - "Che tu possa iniziare la giornata
    con un sorriso." - [KEH too POH-ssah een-YEE-tzah-reh lah johr-NAH-
    tah kohn oon sohr-REE-soh]
20. "Good morning, I hope you have a great day." - "Buon giorno, spero che
    tu abbia un'ottima giornata." - [BWOHN JOHR-no, SPEH-roh keh too
    AHB-byah oh-TEE-mah johr-NAH-tah]
21. "May you meet interesting people today." - "Che tu possa incontrare
    persone interessanti oggi." - [KEH too POH-ssah een-kohn-TRAH-reh
    pehr-SOH-neh een-teh-REHS-sahn-tee OH-jee]
22. "Good morning, remember to enjoy every moment." - "Buon giorno,
    ricorda di goderti ogni istante." - [BWOHN JOHR-no, ree-KOHR-dah
    dee goh-DEHR-tee OH-nee ees-TAHN-teh]
23. "Good morning, may every moment be an opportunity." - "Buon giorno,
    che ogni momento sia un'opportunità." - [BWOHN JOHR-no, keh OH-
    nee moh-MEN-toh see-ah oon-op-por-TOO-nee-tah]
24. "Good morning, may you enjoy the beauty of this day." - "Buon giorno,
    che tu possa goderti la bellezza di questa giornata." - [BWOHN JOHR-
    no, keh too POH-ssah goh-DEHR-tee lah bel-LEH-tzah dee KWEH-
    stah johr-NAH-tah]

WEATHER

COMMON WORDS OF THE WEATHER

1. "Weather" - "Tempo" - [TEM-poh]
2. "Cloud" - "Nuvola" - [NOO-voh-lah]
3. "Sun" - "Sole" - [SOH-leh]
4. "Rain" - "Pioggia" - [PYOH-jah]
5. "Snow" - "Neve" - [NEH-veh]
6. "Wind" - "Vento" - [VEN-toh]
7. "Storm" - "Tempesta" - [TEM-peh-stah]
8. "Forecast" - "Previsione" - [preh-vi-SYO-neh]
9. "Temperature" - "Temperatura" - [tem-peh-rah-TOO-rah]
10. "Humidity" - "Umidità" - [oo-mee-DEE-tah]
11. "Thunder" - "Tuono" - [TOO-oh-noh]
12. "Lightning" - "Fulmine" - [FOOL-mee-neh]
13. "Fog" - "Nebbia" - [NEH-byah]

14. "Heat" - "Calore" - [kah-LOH-reh]
15. "Cold" - "Freddo" - [FREHD-doh]
16. "Warm" - "Caldo" - [KAHL-doh]
17. "Chill" - "Frigido" - [FREE-jee-doh]
18. "Frost" - "Gelo" - [JEH-loh]
19. "Ice" - "Ghiaccio" - [GYAH-chyo]
20. "Hail" - "Grandine" - [GRAN-dee-neh]

PHRASES DESCRIBING WEATHER

1. "What a beautiful sun today!" - "Che bel sole oggi!" - [keh behl SOH-leh OH-jee]
2. "It's hot here!" - "Fa caldo qui!" - [fah KAL-doh kwee]
3. "There's a cool breeze." - "C'è una brezza fresca." - [cheh OO-nah BREHT-zah FREHS-kah]
4. "What a cloudy day!" - "Che giornata nuvolosa!" - [keh jor-NAH-tah noo-voh-LOH-zah]
5. "It's raining heavily!" - "Sta piovendo a dirotto!" - [stah pee-oh-VEHN-doh ah dee-ROHT-toh]
6. "There's fog around." - "C'è nebbia in giro." - [cheh NEHB-byah in JEER-oh]
7. "It's a bit cold." - "Fa un po' freddo." - [fah oon poh FREHD-doh]
8. "The sky is clear." - "Il cielo è sereno." - [eel CHEE-eh-loh eh seh-REH-noh]
9. "Thunderstorms are forecasted today." - "Si prevedono temporali oggi." - [see preh-veh-DOH-noh tem-poh-RAH-lee OH-jee]
10. "It's humid and muggy." - "È umido e afoso." - [eh OO-mee-doh eh ah-FOH-soh]
11. "There's a gentle sea breeze." - "C'è una leggera brezza marina." - [cheh OO-nah leh-JEH-rah BREHT-zah mah-REE-nah]
12. "The sun is shining in the blue sky." - "Il sole splende nel cielo azzurro." - [eel SOH-leh SPLEHN-deh nehll CHEE-eh-loh ah-DZOO-rroh]
13. "It's a cool and breezy day." - "È una giornata fresca e ventilata." - [eh OO-nah jor-NAH-tah FREHS-kah eh ven-tee-LAH-tah]
14. "A heavy snowfall is expected." - "Si prevede un'abbondante nevicata." - [see preh-VEH-deh oon-ahb-bon-DAN-teh neh-vee-KAH-tah]
15. "The wind is blowing strongly today." - "Il vento soffia forte oggi." - [eel VEN-toh SOF-fee-ah FOR-teh OH-jee]
16. "There's a storm coming." - "C'è un temporale in arrivo." - [cheh oon tem-poh-RAH-leh in ah-REE-voh]
17. "The temperature is pleasant." - "La temperatura è piacevole." - [lah tem-peh-rah-TOO-rah eh pyah-cheh-VOH-leh]
18. "It's a humid day with low clouds." - "È un giorno umido con nuvole basse." - [eh oon JOHR-noh OO-mee-doh kohn NOO-voh-leh BAHS-seh]

19. "The climate is mild and pleasant." - "Il clima è mite e piacevole." - [eel KLEE-mah eh MEE-teh eh pyah-cheh-VOH-leh]
20. "There's an overcast sky with gray clouds." - "C'è un cielo coperto di nuvole grigie." - [cheh oon CHEE-eh-loh koh-PEHR-toh dee NOO-voh-leh GREE-dje]

6

BREAKFAST

Breakfast is a special time in Italy, a moment when the family gathers to start the day with joy and good food. It's an opportunity to share precious moments, catch up on news, and engage in pleasant conversations. In this chapter, we will explore a variety of phrases and expressions related to breakfast, from ordering your favorite coffee to discussing delicious Italian pastries. Whether you're enjoying a leisurely meal at home or exploring local cafes, these phrases will help you navigate the breakfast experience like a true Italian. So grab a cup of coffee and get ready to delve into the delightful world of Italian breakfast traditions.

COMMON BREAKFAST FOODS

1. "Coffee and croissant" - "Caffè e croissant" - [KA-fey eh kroh-SAHNT]
2. "Bread and jam" - "Pane e marmellata" - [PAH-neh eh mahr-meh-LAH-tah]
3. "Yogurt and cereal" - "Yogurt e cereali" - [YO-gurt eh cheh-REH-ah-lee]

4. "Scrambled eggs" - "Uova strapazzate" - [OO-oh-vah strah-paht-ZAH-teh]
5. "Pancakes with maple syrup" - "Pancakes con sciroppo d'acero" - [PAN-kayks kohn shee-ROHP-po dah-KEH-roh]
6. "Fresh fruit" - "Frutta fresca" - [FROOT-tah FREHS-kah]
7. "Ham and cheese" - "Prosciutto e formaggio" - [proh-SHOO-toh eh for-MAH-djoh]
8. "Milk and cereal" - "Latte e cereali" - [LAH-teh eh cheh-REH-ah-lee]
9. "Toast with honey" - "Pane tostato con miele" - [PAH-neh toh-STAH-toh kohn MYEH-leh]
10. "Jam tart" - "Crostata alla marmellata" - [kroh-STAH-tah AHL-lah mahr-meh-LAH-tah]
11. "Italian donut" - "Bombolone" - [bom-boh-LOH-neh]
12. "Coffee with milk" - "Caffè con latte" - [KA-fey kohn LAH-teh]
13. "Cream-filled brioche" - "Brioche ripiena di crema" - [bree-OH-keh ree-PYEH-nah dee KREH-mah]
14. "Cornflakes with milk" - "Cornflakes con latte" - [korn-FLEYKS kohn LAH-teh]
15. "Apple pie" - "Torta di mele" - [TOR-tah dee MEH-leh]
16. "Vegetable omelette" - "Frittata di verdure" - [freet-TAH-tah dee vehr-DOO-reh]
17. "Chocolate croissant" - "Cornetto al cioccolato" - [kor-NET-toh ahl choh-koh-LAH-toh]
18. "Crepes with Nutella" - "Crepes con Nutella" - [KREPS kohn noo-TEL-lah]
19. "Hot chocolate" - "Cioccolata calda" - [chohk-koh-LAH-tah KAHL-dah]
20. "Croissant with cream filling" - "Cornetto con ripieno di crema" - [kor-NET-toh kohn ree-PYEH-noh dee KREH-mah]

PHRASES TO SAY AT BREAKFAST

1. "Could I have a cup of coffee, please?" - "Potrei avere una tazza di caffè, per favore?" [POH-trey ah-VEH-reh OO-nah TAH-tsah dee kah-FEH, pehr fah-VOH-reh]
2. "I would like some toast with butter and jam." - "Vorrei del pane tostato con burro e marmellata." [vor-REHY del PAH-neh toh-STAH-toh kohn BOOR-roh eh mar-me-LAH-tah]
3. "Could you pass the sugar?" - "Potresti passarmi lo zucchero?" [poh-TREH-stee pah-SAR-mee loh TSOO-kheh-roh]
4. "May I have a glass of orange juice?" - "Potrei avere un bicchiere di succo d'arancia?" [POH-trey ah-VEH-reh oon bee-KYEH-reh dee SOO-koh dar-RAHN-cha]
5. "Do you have any whole grain cereal?" - "Avete dei cereali integrali?" [ah-VEH-teh day cheh-reh-AH-lee een-teh-GRAH-lee]
6. "I would like a croissant, please." - "Vorrei un cornetto, per favore." [vor-REHY oon kor-NET-toh, pehr fah-VOH-reh]

7. "I prefer tea to coffee in the morning." - "Preferisco il tè al caffè la mattina." [preh-feh-REES-koh eel TEH ahl kah-FEH lah mah-TEE-nah]
8. "Could I have some milk in my coffee?" - "Potrei avere un po' di latte nel mio caffè?" [POH-trey ah-VEH-reh oon po dee LAH-tteh nel MEE-oh kah-FEH]
9. "Do you have any fruit for breakfast?" - "Avete della frutta per colazione?" [ah-VEH-teh DEL-lah FROO-ttah pehr koh-lah-TSYOH-neh]
10. "I am ready for breakfast." - "Sono pronto per la colazione." [SOH-no PRON-toh pehr lah koh-lah-TSYOH-neh]
11. "Could I try the local breakfast?" - "Potrei provare la colazione locale?" [POH-trey pro-VAH-reh lah koh-lah-TSYOH-neh lo- KAH-leh]
12. "Do you serve breakfast all day?" - "Servite la colazione tutto il giorno?" [ser-VEE-teh lah koh-lah-TSYOH-neh TOOT-toh eel JOHR-noh]
13. "Do you have any vegetarian options for breakfast?" - "Avete opzioni vegetariane per la colazione?" [ah-VEH-teh op-TSYOH-nee veh-jeh-TAH-ryah-neh pehr lah koh-lah-TSYOH-neh]
14. "Could I have a second cup of coffee?" - "Potrei avere una seconda tazza di caffè?" [POH-trey ah-VEH-reh OO-nah se-KOHN-dah TAH-tsah dee kah-FEH]
15. "May I have some honey with my tea?" - "Posso avere un po' di miele con il mio tè?" [POH-soh ah-VEH-reh oon poh dee MYEH-leh kohn eel MEE-oh teh]
16. "These pastries look delicious." - "Queste paste sembrano deliziose." [KWEH-steh PAH-steh sem-BRAH-noh deh-lee-TSYOH-zeh]
17. "I love having fresh fruit in the morning." - "Adoro avere frutta fresca la mattina." [ah-DOH-roh ah-VEH-reh FROOT-tah FREHS-kah lah mah-TEE-nah]
18. "Where is the breakfast served?" - "Dove si serve la colazione?" [DOH-veh see SER-veh lah koh-lah-TSYOH-neh]
19. "Could I get an omelette?" - "Potrei avere un'omelette?" [POH-trey ah-VEH-reh oon oh-MEH-let]
20. "I would like some yogurt and granola." - "Vorrei dello yogurt e granola." [vor-REHY DEL-loh YOH-gurt eh grah-NOH-lah]

HOW TO ORDER BREAKFAST AT THE BAR

1. "I would like a coffee and a croissant, please." - "Vorrei un caffè e un cornetto, per favore." [vor-REY oon KA-fey e oon kor-NEH-toh, per fa-VOR-eh]
2. "Can I have a yogurt and cereal?" - "Posso avere uno yogurt e cereali?" [POH-soh a-VEY-rey OO-no yo-GURT e che-re-AH-lee]
3. "Can you bring me a serving of pancakes with maple syrup?" - "Mi porti una porzione di pancake con sciroppo d'acero?" [mi POR-tee OO-na por-TZYO-neh dee PAN-cake kon shee-ROHP-po dah-KEH-ro]

4. "I would like a cup of American coffee, please." - "Desidero una tazza di caffè americano, per cortesia." [de-zi-DEY-ro OO-na TAT-tsah dee KA-fey a-meh-ree-KA-no, per kor-TEH-zee-ah]
5. "I would like a slice of jam tart." - "Vorrei una fetta di crostata di marmellata." [vor-REY OO-na FET-tah dee kro-STAH-tah dee mar-mel-LAH-tah]
6. "Give me a cappuccino with a cream-filled brioche, please." - "Mi dia un cappuccino con una brioche alla crema." [mi DYA oon kap-poo-CHEE-no kon OO-na bree-OH-keh AHL-la KREH-mah]
7. "Can I order some toast with honey?" - "Posso ordinare delle fette biscottate con miele?" [POH-soh oor-di-NA-rey DEL-le FET-te be-sko-TAH-te kon MEE-leh]
8. "Can you recommend an apple pie?" - "Mi consiglia una torta di mele?" [mi kon-SY-lya OO-na TOR-ta dee MEH-leh]
9. "I would like a donut and a coffee with milk, thank you." - "Vorrei una ciambella e un caffellatte, grazie." [vor-REY OO-na cham-BEL-la e oon ka-fe-lla-TAY, GRA-tsyeh]
10. "Can you bring me a chocolate croissant, please?" - "Mi porti un cornetto al cioccolato, per cortesia?" [mi POR-tee oon kor-NEH-to al cho-co-LAH-to, per kor-TEH-zee-ah]

SUPERMARKET

COMMON SUPERMARKET WORDS

1. "Groceries" - "Spesa" - [SPEH-zah]
2. "Cart" - "Carrello" - [kar-REHL-loh]
3. "Checkout" - "Cassa" - [KAH-sah]
4. "Aisle" - "Corsia" - [KOR-syah]
5. "Produce" - "Prodotti freschi" - [pro-DOH-tee FREH-skee]
6. "Dairy" - "Latticini" - [laht-tee-CHEE-nee]
7. "Bakery" - "Panetteria" - [pah-net-TEH-ryah]
8. "Frozen" - "Surgelati" - [soor-geh-LAH-tee]
9. "Canned" - "In scatola" - [in ska-TOH-lah]
10. "Meat" - "Carne" - [KAR-neh]
11. "Fish" - "Pesce" - [PEH-sheh]
12. "Beverages" - "Bibite" - [bee-BEE-teh]
13. "Snacks" - "Snacks" - [snacks]

14. "Cleaning products" - "Prodotti per la pulizia" - [pro-DOH-tee pehr lah poo-LEE-tsyah]
15. "Cosmetics" - "Cosmetici" - [kohs-MEH-tee-chee]
16. "Discount" - "Sconto" - [SKON-toh]
17. "Special offer" - "Offerta speciale" - [of-FER-tah speh-CHAH-leh]
18. "Receipt" - "Scontrino" - [skon-TREE-noh]
19. "Cashier" - "Cassiera" - [kahs-SYEH-rah]
20. "Bag" - "Borsa" - [BOR-sah]

USEFUL PHRASES IN THE SUPERMARKET

1. "Can you bring me a chocolate croissant, please?" - "Mi porti un cornetto al cioccolato, per cortesia?" [mi POR-tee oon kor-NEH-to al cho-co-LAH-to, per kor-TEH-zee-ah]
2. "Where is the dairy section?" - "Dov'è il reparto dei latticini?" [DOH-veh eel reh-PAR-toh dee laht-tee-CHEE-nee?]
3. "Excuse me, where can I find fresh bread?" - "Mi scusi, dove posso trovare il pane fresco?" [Mee SKOO-zee, DOH-veh POSS-oh troh-VAH-rey eel PAH-neh FRES-ko?]
4. "Do you have eggs in the fresh produce section?" - "Avete le uova nel reparto dei prodotti freschi?" [AH-veh-tey ley OO-oh-vah nel reh-PAR-toh dee pro-DOT-tee FRES-kee?]
5. Can I pay with a credit card?" - "Posso pagare con la carta di credito?" [POHS-soh pah-GA-rey kon lah KAHR-ta dee CREH-dee-toh?]
6. "Excuse me, is there a special offer on this product?" - "Mi scusi, c'è un'offerta speciale su questo prodotto?" [Mee SKOO-zee, c'è oon-off-ER-tah speh-TSYA-leh soo QUE-sto pro-DOHT-to?]
7. "How much does this fruit cost?" - "Quanto costa questa frutta?" [KWAHN-toh KO-sta KWE-sta FROO-ta?]
8. "Where can I find the vegetable section?" - "Dove posso trovare il reparto delle verdure?" [DOH-veh POSS-oh troh-VAH-rey eel reh-PAR-toh DEL-le ver-DOO-rey?]
9. "Excuse me, which line do I take for the checkout?" - "Mi scusi, quale fila devo prendere per il controllo delle cassa?" [Mee SKOO-zee, KWA-leh FEE-la DE-vo pren-DE-rey per eel kon-TRO-lo DEL-le KAS-sa?]
10. "Do you have this product available?" - "Hai questo prodotto disponibile?" [AH-ee KWE-sto pro-DOHT-to DEES-po-NEE-beh-leh?]
11. "Can you help me find the frozen foods?" - "Mi può aiutare a trovare i surgelati?" [Mee PWOH a-yoo-TA-rey a troh-VAH-rey ee soor-ge-LAH-tee?]

8

WORK

Welcome to the chapter dedicated to the workplace, where we will equip you with essential phrases to navigate the professional environment in Italian. These phrases will help you speak clearly and develop strong professional relationships in every work environment, from an office to a café.Greeting coworkers, asking for help, discussing work, and dealing with typical workplace issues are all covered in this section. Mastering these phrases will not only enhance your language skills but also boost your confidence in the workplace.

From job interviews to team meetings and daily interactions, this chapter covers a wide range of workplace scenarios. Get ready to improve your Italian language skills and excel in your professional endeavors!

BASIC TERMINOLOGY OF THE WORKPLACE

1. "Office" - "Ufficio" - [oof-FEE-choh]
2. "Desk" - "Scrivania" - [skri-VAH-nyah]
3. "Computer" - "Computer" - [kom-POO-ter]

4. "Meeting" - "Riunione" - [ryoo-NYO-neh]
5. "Boss" - "Capo" - [KAH-poh]
6. "Employee" - "Dipendente" - [dee-pen-DEN-teh]
7. "Printer" - "Stampante" - [stam-PAN-teh]
8. "Email" - "Email" - [E-mail]
9. "Document" - "Documento" - [do-ku-MEN-toh]
10. "Fax" - "Fax" - [fax]
11. "Telephone" - "Telefono" - [teh-LEH-foh-noh]
12. "File" - "File" - [FEE-leh]
13. "Pen" - "Penna" - [PEN-nah]
14. "Stapler" - "Cucitrice" - [koo-CHEE-tree-cheh]
15. "Notebook" - "Quaderno" - [qua-DEHR-noh]
16. "Agenda" - "Agenda" - [ah-JEN-dah]
17. "Coffee break" - "Pausa caffè" - [PAH-oo-sah kah-FEH]
18. "Project" - "Progetto" - [pro-JET-toh]
19. "Deadline" - "Scadenza" - [sca-DEN-tsa]
20. "Client" - "Cliente" - [KLEE-en-teh]

COMMON INTERACTIONS WITH COLLEAGUES

1. "Could you send me the file?" - "Potresti mandarmi il file?" [poh-TREH-stee mahn-DAR-mee eel fee-leh]
2. "When is the meeting?" - "Quando è la riunione?" [KWAN-doh eh lah ree-YOO-nyoh-neh]
3. "We need to finish the project by the deadline." - "Dobbiamo finire il progetto per la scadenza." [DOHB-byah-moh fee-NEE-reh eel pro-JET-toh pehr lah sca-DEN-tsa]
4. "I'll send you an email." - "Ti manderò un'email." [tee mahn-deh-ROH oon e-mail]
5. "The printer is out of ink." - "La stampante è senza inchiostro." [lah stam-PAN-teh eh SEHN-zah in-KYO-stroh]
6. "I need a break." - "Ho bisogno di una pausa." [oh bee-ZOH-nyoh dee OO-nah PAH-oo-sah]
7. "Please, could you fix the computer?" - "Per favore, potresti sistemare il computer?" [pehr fa-VOH-reh, poh-TREH-stee see-steh-MAH-reh eel kom-POO-ter]
8. "Where is my desk?" - "Dov'è la mia scrivania?" [doh-VEH lah MEE-ah skri-VAH-nyah]
9. "We have a new client." - "Abbiamo un nuovo cliente." [ahb-BYAH-moh oon NOO-voh KLEE-en-teh]
10. "Can you answer the phone?" - "Puoi rispondere al telefono?" [PWOH-ee ree-SPON-deh-reh al teh-LEH-foh-noh]
11. "We need to discuss this in the meeting." - "Dobbiamo discuterne nella riunione." [DOHB-byah-moh dees-koo-TEHR-neh NEHL-lah ree-YOO-nyoh-neh]

12. "Could you update the document?" - "Potresti aggiornare il documento?" [poh-TREH-stee ah-johr-NAH-reh eel doh-koo-MEN-toh]
13. "The boss wants to see you." - "Il capo vuole vederti." [eel KAH-poh VWOH-leh veh-DEHR-tee]
14. "Who is responsible for this project?" - "Chi è responsabile di questo progetto?" [kee eh reh-spon-SAH-bee-leh dee KWEH-stoh pro-JET-toh]
15. "Please, make a copy of these files." - "Per favore, fai una copia di questi file." [pehr fa-VOH-reh, fah-EE OO-nah KOH-pyah dee KWEH-stee fee-leh]
16. "I left a message for you." - "Ho lasciato un messaggio per te." [oh lah-SHAH-toh oon meh-SAH-joh pehr teh]
17. "Do we have enough office supplies?" - "Abbiamo abbastanza materiale d'ufficio?" [ahb-BYAH-moh ab-bah-STAHN-tsah ma-teh-ryah-leh doof-FEE-choh]
18. "When is the deadline for this task?" - "Quando è la scadenza per questo compito?" [KWAN-doh eh lah sca-DEN-tsa pehr KWEH-stoh kohm-PEE-toh]
19. "Let's have a coffee break." - "Facciamo una pausa caffè." [fah-CHAH-moh OO-nah PAH-oo-sah kah-FEH]
20. "I'll check the fax." - "Controllo il fax." [kon-TROH-loh eel fax]

TALK TO YOUR BOSS

1. "I would like to get your opinion on the current status of the project." - "Vorrei avere il suo parere sullo stato attuale del progetto." [Vohr-ray ah-veh-ray eel soo-oh pah-ray-reh sohl-loh stah-toh aht-too-ah-leh del pro-yet-to]
2. "I have some ideas that could contribute to the success of the project." - "Ho alcune idee che potrebbero contribuire al successo del progetto." [Oh ahl-koo-neh ee-deh keh po-trehb-beh-roh kon-tree-boo-ee-reh ahl soo-ches-soh del pro-yet-to]
3. "I would like to share with you the progress we have made so far." - "Vorrei condividere con lei i progressi che abbiamo fatto finora." [Vohr-ray kon-dee-veh-reh kon lay ee proh-grehs-see keh ahb-bia-moh fah-toh fee-noh-rah]
4. "I would like to get your opinion on this issue." - "Mi piacerebbe avere il suo parere su questa questione." [Mee pee-ah-cheh-reh ah-veh-ray eel soo-oh pah-ray-reh soo kweh-stee-oh-neh]
5. "I would like to get your opinion on the current status of the project." - "Vorrei avere il suo parere sullo stato attuale del progetto." [Vor-REY ah-VEH-ray eel soo-OH par-ER-eh soo-LOH stah-TOH at-too-AH-lay del pro-JET-to]
6. "I have some ideas that could contribute to the success of the project." - "Ho alcune idee che potrebbero contribuire al successo del progetto." [Oh al-KOO-nay ee-DEH-kay po-treb-BRO con-tree-BOO-ree al soo-CHESS-oh del pro-JET-to]

7. "I would like to share with you the progress we have made so far." - "Vorrei condividere con lei i progressi che abbiamo fatto finora." [Vor-REY con-dee-VEH-ray con lay ee pro-GRESS-ee kay ab-BEE-amo FAH-toh fee-NOR-ah]

8. "I would like to get your opinion on this issue." - "Mi piacerebbe avere il suo parere su questa questione." [Mee pee-a-CHEH-reh-bay ah-VEH-ray eel soo-OH par-ER-eh soo KWES-tah ques-TYO-neh]

9. "I would like to better understand what the company's goals and expectations are." - "Vorrei capire meglio quali sono gli obiettivi dell'azienda e le sue aspettative." [Vor-REY cah-PEER-eh MEG-lee-OH kwah-LEE son-oh glee ob-yet-TEE-vee dell-ah-tsee-YEN-dah eh leh soo-eh ass-pet-TAH-tee-veh]

10. "We need more resources to move the project forward." - "Abbiamo bisogno di più risorse per portare avanti il progetto." [Ahb-BEE-amo bee-ZON-yoh dee pyoo ree-SOR-seh pair por-TAH-ray ah-VAN-tee eel pro-JET-to]

11. "I developed a proposal to optimize our internal processes." - "Ho sviluppato una proposta per ottimizzare i nostri processi interni." [Oh svil-LOO-pah-toh OOH-nah pro-PO-stah pair ot-tee-MEE-tzee-are-eh ee NO-stree pro-CHESS-ee in-TER-nee]

12. "There is a critical problem that needs our immediate attention." - "C'è un problema critico che richiede la nostra attenzione immediata." [Cheh oon pro-BLEM-ah cree-TEE-coh kay ree-kye-DEH lah NO-strah at-ten-tsyoh-NEH ee-mee-dee-AH-tah]

13. "I am grateful for your support and trust in me." - "Sono grato per il suo sostegno e la fiducia che ha riposto in me." [SO-noh GRA-toh pair eel soo-OH sos-TEG-noh eh lah fee-DOO-kia kay ah ree-PO-stoh in meh]

14. "Can I attend the meeting?" - "Posso partecipare alla riunione?" [POS-soh par-teh-chee-PAH-ray ahllah ree-yoo-nee-OH-neh]

15. "Where will the meeting be held and at what time?" - "Dove si terrà la riunione e a che ora?" [DOH-veh see teh-RAH lah ree-yoo-nee-OH-neh eh ah keh OR-ah]

16. "I am available to attend the meeting." - "Sono disponibile a partecipare alla riunione." [SO-noh dee-spoh-NEE-bee-leh ah par-teh-chee-PAH-ray ahllah ree-yoo-nee-OH-neh]

17. "Can we have an agenda for the meeting?" - "Possiamo avere un ordine del giorno per la riunione?" [Pos-see-AH-moh ah-VEH-reh oon or-DEE-neh del JOR-noh pair lah ree-yoo-nee-OH-neh]

18. "I confirm my participation in the meeting." - "Confermo la mia partecipazione alla riunione." [Con-FER-moh lah mee-AH par-teh-chee-pah-TSEE-oh-neh ahllah ree-yoo-nee-OH-neh]

19. "Could you provide more details about the meeting?" - "Potresti fornire ulteriori dettagli sulla riunione?" [Pot-RES-tee for-NEE-reh ool-tee-oh-REE dee-TAH-lyee soo-lah ree-yoo-nee-OH-neh]

20. "Should we prepare something for the meeting?" - "Dobbiamo preparare qualcosa per la riunione?" [Dohb-BEE-amo preh-PAH-ray kwa-LOH-sah pair lah ree-yoo-nee-OH-neh]
21. "I am ready to give my input during the meeting." - "Sono pronto a dare il mio contributo durante la riunione." [SO-noh PRON-toh ah DAH-ray eel MEE-oh con-TRI-boo-toh doo-RAN-teh lah ree-yoo-nee-OH-neh]
22. "What is the format or purpose of the meeting?" - "Qual è il formato o lo scopo della riunione?" [KWAL eh eel for-MAH-toh oh loh SKO-po dell-ah ree-yoo-nee-OH-neh]
23. "Thank you for the invitation to the meeting." - "Grazie per l'invito alla riunione." [Grah-TSYEH pair lin-VEE-toh ahllah ree-yoo-nee-OH-neh]

9

EATING

People congregate during lunchtime in Italy to experience the exquisite aromas of Italian cuisine, nibble on an appetizer while taking a respite from the rush and bustle of the city streets, and drink beverages such as Spritz (which I highly recommend trying out).

Let's delve into the art of placing orders at an Italian restaurant.

Get ready, because once in Italy you will be able to confidently consult the menu of the fine restaurants you will try, participating in a truly authentic culinary experience.

COMMON WORDS RELATING TO MEALS

1. "Lunch" - "Pranzo" - [PRAHN-tsoh]
2. "Dinner" - "Cena" - [CHEH-nah]
3. "Dishes" - "Piatti" - [PYAHT-tee]
4. "Table" - "Tavolo" - [TAH-voh-loh]
5. "Kitchen" - "Cucina" - [koo-CHEE-nah]

6. "Menu" - "Menu" - [MEH-noo]
7. "Appetizer" - "Antipasto" - [ahn-tee-PAH-stoh]
8. "First course" - "Primo" - [PREE-moh]
9. "Second course" - "Secondo" - [seh-KOHN-doh]
10. "Dessert" - "Dolce" - [DOHL-cheh]
11. "Beverage" - "Bevanda" - [be-VAHN-dah]
12. "Wine" - "Vino" - [VEE-noh]
13. "Beer" - "Birra" - [BEER-rah]
14. "Bread" - "Pane" - [PAH-neh]
15. "Salad" - "Insalata" - [een-sah-LAH-tah]
16. "Meat" - "Carne" - [KAHR-neh]
17. "Fish" - "Pesce" - [PEH-sheh]
18. "Vegetables" - "Verdure" - [ver-DOO-reh]
19. "Cheese" - "Formaggio" - [for-MAH-djoh]
20. "Fruit" - "Frutta" - [FROOT-tah]

MENU VOCABULARY

1. "I would like to see the menu, please." - "Vorrei vedere il menu, per favore." [Vor-rey ve-DE-rey eel MEH-noo, per fa-VO-re.]
2. "What are the specials of the day?" - "Quali sono le specialità del giorno?" [KWA-lee SO-no le spe-tsee-A-lee del GO-rno?]
3. "Do you have any vegetarian options?" - "Avete opzioni vegetariane?" [A-VE-teh OP-tsee-o-nee ve-ge-ta-RI-a-neh?]
4. "What is your recommendation?" - "Qual è la vostra raccomandazione?" [KWAHL eh la VOS-tra ra-koh-man-da-TSYO- neh?]
5. "I'll have the lasagna, please." - "Prendo la lasagna, per favore." [PREN-do la la-ZA-nya, per fa-VO-re.]
6. "Is there a children's menu available?" - "C'è un menu per bambini disponibile?" [Cheh oon MEH-noo per bam-BEE-nee dis-po-NEE-bee-leh?]
7. "Can I have a glass of water, please?" - "Posso avere un bicchiere d'acqua, per favore?" [POSS-so a-VE-rey oon beek-KYEH-rey DA-kwa, per fa-VO-re?]
8. "I'd like my steak medium-rare." - "Vorrei la mia bistecca al sangue." [Vor-rey la MEE-a be-STEK-ka al SAN-gweh.]
9. "Can you recommend a local specialty?" - "Puoi consigliare una specialità locale?" [POO-oy kon-see-LYAH-rey OO-na spe-tsya-lee-TA lo-KA-leh?]
10. "Is there a dessert menu available?" - "C'è un menu dei dolci disponibile?" [Cheh oon MEH-noo dei DOL-chee dis-po-NEE-bee-leh?]

1. "What do you recommend for the main course?" - "Cosa mi consiglia per il secondo piatto?" [KOH-sa mee kon-SYE-lya per eel se-KON-do PYA-tto?]
2. "Can you suggest a good wine pairing?" - "Può suggerirmi un buon abbinamento di vino?" [POO-oh sood-jer-EER-mee oon BWON ab-bee-na-MEN-to dee VEE-no?]
3. "Is the pasta homemade?" - "La pasta è fatta in casa?" [La PA-sta eh FAT-ta een KA-sa?]
4. "What is the chef's specialty?" - "Qual è la specialità dello chef?" [KWAHL eh la spe-tsyah-lee-TA del-LO chef?]
5. "Do you have any local dishes on the menu?" - "Avete piatti tipici della zona nel menu?" [A-VE-te pee-AHT-tee TEE-pee-chee DEL-la ZO-na nel MEH-noo?]
6. "Can I customize my order?" - "Posso personalizzare il mio ordine?" [POSS-so per-so-na-lee-ZA-rey eel MEE-o or-DEE-ney?]
7. "Are there any vegetarian options available?" - "Ci sono opzioni vegetariane disponibili?" [Chee SO-no OP-tsee-O-nee ve-ge-ta-RYA-neh dis-po-NEE-bee-lee?]
8. "What is the portion size like?" - "Com'è la dimensione delle porzioni?" [KOM-eh la dee-men-ZYO-ney DEY-ley por-TSYO-nee?]
9. "Can you make it spicy?" - "Può renderlo piccante?" [POO-oh ren-DER-lo pee-CAN-te?]
10. "What desserts do you recommend?" - "Quali dolci mi consiglia?" [KWA-lee DOL-chee mee kon-SYE-lya?]

PHRASES TO EXPRESS FOOD PREFERENCES AND ALLERGIES

1. "Are there any gluten-free options?" - "Ci sono opzioni senza glutine?" [Chee SO-no OP-tsee-O-nee SEN-za gloo-TEE-neh?]
2. "I'm allergic to nuts." - "Sono allergico alle noci." [SO-no al-ler-GEE-ko AL-le NO-chee.]
3. "Can you make it without dairy?" - "Può farlo senza latticini?" [POO-oh FAR-lo SEN-za lat-tee-CHEE-nee?]
4. "Can I substitute the side dish?" - "Posso sostituire il contorno?" [POSS-so so-sti-TWEE-rey eel kon-TOR-no?]
5. "Do you have any vegan options? - "Avete opzioni vegane?" [A-VE-te op-TSYO-nee ve-GA-ne?]
6. "Can you make it with less salt?" - "Può farlo con meno sale?" [POO-oh FAR-lo kon MEH-no SA-le?]
7. "I'm vegetarian, so no meat or fish, please." - "Sono vegetariano, quindi niente carne né pesce, per favore." [SO-no ve-ge-ta-RYA-no, KWIN-dye NYEN-te CAR-ney ne PE-she, per fa-VO-re.]

8. "I'm on a gluten-free diet." - "Seguo una dieta senza glutine." [SE-gwo OO-na DEY-ta SEN-za gloo-TEE-neh.]
9. "Can I have the dressing on the side, please?" - "Posso avere il condimento a parte, per favore?" [POSS-so a-VE-re eel kon-dee-MEN-to a PAR-te, per fa-VO-re?]
10. "Are there any vegetarian sauces available?" - "Ci sono salse vegetariane disponibili?" [Chee SO-no SAL-se ve-ge-ta-RYA-ne dis-po-NEE-bee-lee?]

BILL TIME

1. "Could I have the bill, please?" - "Posso avere il conto, per favore?" [POHS-soh ah-VEH-reh eel KON-toh, pehr fah-VOH-reh?]
2. "Can we split the bill?" - "Possiamo dividere il conto?" [POHS-see-ah-moh dee-VEE-deh-reh eel KON-toh?]
3. "I'd like to pay by credit card." - "Vorrei pagare con la carta di credito." [VOR-reh-ee pah-GAH-reh kohn lah KAHR-tah dee KREH-dee-toh.]
4. "Do you accept cash?" - "Accettate contanti?" [A-chet-TAH-teh kohn-TAHN-tee?]
5. "Could you bring the card machine?" - "Potresti portare il pos?" [Poh-TRES-tee pohr-TAH-reh eel POS?]
6. "Can I pay with a different currency?" - "Posso pagare con una valuta diversa?" [POHS-soh pah-GAH-reh kohn OO-nah vah-LOO-tah dee-VEH-rah?]
7. "I'd like a receipt, please." - "Vorrei una ricevuta, per favore." [VOR-reh-ee OO-nah ree-cheh-VOO-tah, pehr fah-VOH-reh.]
8. "What's the total amount, including tax?" - "Qual è l'importo totale, tasse incluse?" [KWAL eh leem-POH-toh toh-TAH-leh, TAS-seh een-KLOO-zeh?]
9. "Is service included in the bill?" - "Il servizio è incluso nel conto?" [Eel sehr-VEE-tsyoh eh een-KLOO-soh nel KON-toh?]

EXPLORING THE CITY

Confronting with unexpected surroundings and navigating a new city can be an exhilarating experience, but it also has the potential to be overwhelming.

This chapter is your guide to exploring an Italian city with ease.

Whether you're wandering through ancient streets or hopping on public transportation, having the right phrases at your disposal is essential.

Acquire the skills necessary to converse with people, ask for directions, locate the closest attractions, place food orders at local restaurants, and navigate your way about.

With this comprehensive resource, you'll navigate the city like a seasoned traveler, uncovering hidden gems and immersing yourself in the vibrant culture of Italy's urban landscapes.

Get ready to embark on a memorable adventure!

Here are the most common words for travel:

1. "Right" - "Destra" - [DEH-strah]
2. "Left" - "Sinistra" - [see-NEES-trah]

3. "Forward" - "Avanti" - [ah-VAHN-tee]
4. "Backward" - "Indietro" - [in-DYEH-troh]
5. "High" - "Alto" - [AHL-toh]
6. "Low" - "Basso" - [BAHS-soh]
7. "Near" - "Vicino" - [vee-CHEE-noh]
8. "Far" - "Lontano" - [lohn-TAH-noh]
9. "In front" - "Davanti" - [dah-VAHN-tee]
10. "Behind" - "Dietro" - [DYEH-troh]
11. "Above" - "Sopra" - [SOH-prah]
12. "Below" - "Sotto" - [SOHT-toh]
13. "At the corner" - "All'angolo" - [ahl-LAHN-goh-loh]
14. "Across" - "Attraverso" - [at-tra-VER-soh]
15. "Straight" - "Dritto" - [DREE-toh]
16. "Curve" - "Curva" - [KOOR-vah]
17. "Sign" - "Segnale" - [seh-GNAH-leh]
18. "Intersection" - "Incrocio" - [een-KROH-choh]
19. "Roundabout" - "Rotatoria" - [roh-tah-TOH-ree-ah]
20. "Stop" - "Fermata" - [fehr-MAH-tah]
21. "Route" - "Percorso" - [per-KOR-so]
22. "Road" - "Strada" - [STRAH-dah]
23. "Highway" - "Autostrada" - [ow-toh-STRAH-dah]
24. "Pedestrian" - "Pedonale" - [peh-doh-NAH-leh]
25. "Traffic light" - "Semafaro" - [seh-mah-FAH-roh]
26. "Signpost" - "Cartello" - [kar-TEL-loh]
27. "Direction" - "Direzione" - [dee-reh-TSYOH-neh]
28. "Exit" - "Uscita" - [oo-SHEE-tah]
29. "Entrance" - "Ingresso" - [een-GREHS-soh]
30. "Roundabout" - "Rotonda" - [roh-TON-dah]
31. "Detour" - "Deviazione" - [deh-vyah-TSYOH-neh]
32. "Pedestrian crossing" - "Attraversamento pedonale" - [aht-trah-vehr-sah-MEN-to peh-doh-NAH-leh]
33. "Lane" - "Corsia" - [KOR-syah]
34. "Parking" - "Parcheggio" - [par-KEH-joh]
35. "One way" - "Senso unico" - [SEN-soo OO-nee-koh]
36. "Restricted traffic zone" - "Zona a traffico limitato" - [ZO-nah ah trahf-FI-koh lee-mee-TAH-toh]
37. "No parking" - "Divieto di sosta" - [dee-VYEH-toh dee SOH-stah]
38. "Road sign" - "Cartello stradale" - [kar-TEL-lo strah-DAH-leh]
39. "Path" - "Sentiero" - [sen-TYEH-roh]
40. "Landmark" - "Punto di riferimento" - [POON-toh dee ree-feh-REE-men-toh]

ASK FOR AND UNDERSTAND DIRECTIONS

1. "Excuse me, where is the nearest train station?" - "Scusi, dov'è la stazione dei treni?" [skoo-zee, doh-VEH lah stah-zee-YOH-nay trayn-ee?]
2. "Can you tell me how to get to the city center?" - "Può dirmi come arrivare al centro città?" [pwò DEER-mee koh-meh ar-ree-VAH-ray ahl CHEN-tro cheet-TAH?]
3. "Is the museum far from here?" - "Il museo è lontano da qui?" [eel moo-ZAY-oh eh lon-TAH-noh dah kwee?]
4. "Which bus should I take to go to the beach?" - "Quale autobus devo prendere per andare alla spiaggia?" [KWAH-lay ow-TOH-boos DAY-vo pren-DAY-ray per an-DAH-ray AHL-lah spyahg-YAH?]
5. "Excuse me, how do I reach the main square?" - "Scusi, come arrivo alla piazza principale?" [skoo-zee, koh-meh ar-REE-vo AHL-lah pee-AHT-sah preen-chee-PAH-lay?]
6. "Can you show me on the map?" - "Può mostrarmelo sulla mappa?" [pwò mohs-TRAHR-may-lo soo-LAH MAHP-pah?]
7. "Is it better to walk or take a taxi?" - "È meglio camminare o prendere un taxi?" [eh MEH-lyoh kahm-mee-NAH-ray oh pren-DAY-ray o TAHK-see?]
8. "Where can I find a pharmacy?" - "Dove posso trovare una farmacia?" [DOH-vay POH-soh troh-VAH-ray OO-nah fahr-MAH-chee-ah?]
9. "Excuse me, is there a post office nearby?" - "Scusi, c'è un ufficio postale qui vicino?" [skoo-zee, cheh oof-FEE-chee-oh pohs-TAH-lay kwee vee-CHEE-noh?]
10. "Could you please repeat that?" - "Potrebbe ripetere, per favore?" [poh-TREE-beh ree-peh-TAY-ray, per fah-VOH-ray?]
11. "What time does the next bus/train arrive?" - "A che ora arriva il prossimo autobus/treno?" [ah keh OH-rah ah-REE-vah eel PROS-si-mo ow-TOH-boos/TREY-noh?]
12. "Is this the right bus/train to go to the city center?" - "Questo è l'autobus/il treno giusto per andare al centro città?" [KWES-toh eh low-TOH-boos/eel TREY-noh JWOH-sto per an-DAH-ray ahl CHEN-tro cheet-TAH?]
13. "Where is the nearest bus/train stop?" - "Dove si trova la fermata dell'autobus/del treno più vicina?" [DOH-veh see TROH-vah lah fer-MAH-tah del low-TOH-boos/del TREY-noh pyoo vee-CHEE-nah?]
14. "How much does a ticket to the city center cost?" - "Quanto costa un biglietto per il centro città?" [KWAHN-toh COH-stah oon beel-LYET-toh per eel CHEN-tro cheet-TAH?]
15. "Can I use the same ticket for multiple rides?" - "Posso usare lo stesso biglietto per più corse?" [POHS-soh oo-SAH-ray lo STES-so beel-LYET-toh per pwoo KOR-say?]
16. "Excuse me, which platform does the train to (destination) depart from?" - "Scusi, da quale binario parte il treno per (destinazione)?" [SKOO-zee, dah KWAH-leh bee-NAH-ree-oh PAR-tay eel TREY-noh per DESTINATION?]

17. "Are there any discounts available for students/seniors?" - "Ci sono sconti disponibili per studenti/anziani?" [Chee SO-no SKON-tee dees-po-NEE-bee-lee per stoo-DEN-tee/an-TSYAH-nee?]
18. "How often do buses/trains run in this area?" - "Con quale frequenza passano gli autobus/i treni in questa zona?" [KON KWAH-leh froo-WEN-tsa pah-SAH-no gleel ow-TOH-boos/ee TREY-nee een KWEH-sta ZOH-nah?]
19. "Is there a direct bus/train to (destination)?" - "C'è un autobus/un treno diretto per (destinazione)?" [Cheh oon ow-TOH-boos/oon TREY-noh dee-REHT-toh per (des-tee-NAH-tsyoh-neh)?]
20. "Can you tell me where to get off for (landmark/attraction)?" - "Mi può dire dove scendere per (luogo di interesse)?" [Mee pwoh DEE-ray DOH-veh SHEN-deh-ray per (PLACE)?]

INTERACT WITH THE TOUR GUIDE

1. "Can you recommend any guided tours in the city?" - "Può consigliarmi qualche tour guidato nella città?" [PWOH kohn-seel-YAR-mee KW2AHL-kweh toor gwee-DAH-toh NEL-lah chee-TAH?]
2. "How long does the guided tour last?" - "Quanto dura il tour guidato?" [KWAHN-toh DOO-rah eel toor gwee-DAH-toh?]
3. "What is the cost of the guided tour? - "Qual è il costo del tour guidato?" [KWAHL eh eel COHS-toh del toor gwee-DAH-toh?]
4. "Is there an audio guide available in different languages?" - "È disponibile una guida audio in diverse lingue?" [EH dees-po-NEE-bee-leh OO-nah GWEED-ah OW-dee-oh een DEE-ver-seh LEEN-gweh?]
5. "Can you tell me more about the historical sites we will visit?" - "Mi può parlare di più sui siti storici che visiteremo?" [Mee pwoh pahr-LAH-ray dee PEE soo-ee SEE-tee STO-ree-cheh kee vee-see-teh-REH-moh?]
6. "Are there any specific rules or guidelines we should follow during the guided tour?" - "Ci sono regole o linee guida specifiche da seguire durante il tour guidato?" [Chee SO-no reh-GOH-leh o LEE-neh GWEED-ah spee-FEE-keh dah seh-GWEE-ray doo-RAN-tay eel toor gwee-DAH-toh?]
7. "Can we ask questions during the guided tour?" - "Possiamo fare domande durante il tour guidato?" [Pos-SYAH-mo FAH-reh doh-MAHN-deh doo-RAN-tay eel toor gwee-DAH-toh?]"
8. "How can we book a guided tour?" - "Come possiamo prenotare un tour guidato?" [KO-meh pos-SYAH-mo preh-no-TAH-ray oon toor gwee-DAH-toh?]
9. "Is there a dress code for the guided tour?" - "C'è un codice di abbigliamento per il tour guidato?" [Cheh oon koh-DEE-cheh dee ab-bee-LYAH-men-toh per eel toor gwee-DAH-toh?]
10. "Can you provide us with a map or brochure of the guided tour?" - "Può fornirci una mappa o un opuscolo del tour guidato?" [PWOH for-

NEER-chee OO-nah MAHP-pah o oon oh-POOS-koh-lo del toor gwee-DAH-toh?]

DESCRIBE PLACES AND MONUMENTS

1. "The cathedral is a magnificent example of Gothic architecture." - "La cattedrale è un magnifico esempio di architettura gotica." [lah kah-TEH-drah-leh eh oon mahg-NEE-fee-koh eh-KSAYM-pyoh dee ar-kee-TEH-toor-ah goh-TEE-kah.]
2. "The ancient ruins are a testament to the city's rich history." - "Le antiche rovine sono una testimonianza della ricca storia della città." [leh ahn-TEE-keh roo-VEE-neh SO-no OO-nah teh-stee-moh-NEE-ahn-tsah dee-LAH REEK-kah STOH-ree-ah DEHL-lah cheet-TAH.]
3. "The panoramic view from the hilltop is breathtaking." - "La vista panoramica dalla cima della collina è mozzafiato." [lah VEE-stah pah-noh-rah-MEE-kah DAHL-lah CHEE-mah DEHL-lah kohl-LEE-nah eh moht-tsah-FYAH-toh.]
4. "The art museum houses a remarkable collection of masterpieces." - "Il museo d'arte ospita una notevole collezione di capolavori." [eel moo-ZEH-oh DAR-teh oh-SPY-tah OO-nah noh-teh-VOH-leh kohl-leh-TSYOH-neh dee kah-poh-lah-VOH-ree.]
5. "The historic square is bustling with activity and lined with charming cafes." - "La piazza storica è vivace di attività e costellata di affascinanti caffè." [lah pee-AHTS-sah STOH-ree-kah eh vee-VAH-cheh dee aht-tee-VEE-tah ee koh-stel-LAH-tah dee ahf-fah-shi-NAHN-tee KAH-feh.]
6. "The castle stands as a symbol of the city's medieval past." - "Il castello si erge come simbolo del passato medievale della città." [eel kah-STEL-lo see AYR-jeh KOH-meh SEEM-boh-lo del pah-SAH-toh meh-dee-EH-vah-leh DEHL-lah cheet-TAH.]
7. "The vibrant market offers a variety of local produce and handmade crafts." - "Il mercato vivace offre una varietà di prodotti locali e artigianato fatto a mano." [eel mer-KAH-to vee-VAH-cheh OHF-freh OO-nah vah-ree-EH-tah dee pro-DOHT-tee loh-KAH-lee eh ar-tee-jah-NAH-toh FAHT-toh ah MAH-no.]
8. "The charming alleyways are perfect for leisurely strolls." - "I suggestivi vicoli sono perfetti per piacevoli passeggiate." [ee soos-TEE-vee vee-KOH-lee SO-no per-FET-tee per pyah-cheh-VOH-lee pah-seh-DJAH-tee.]
9. "The park is an oasis of tranquility in the heart of the city." - "Il parco è un'oasi di tranquillità nel cuore della città." [eel PAR-koh eh oon wah-ZEE dee trahn-kwee-LEE-tah nel KWOH-reh DEL-lah cheet-TAH.]
10. "The architectural details of the buildings are stunning." - "I dettagli architettonici degli edifici sono sbalorditivi." [ee det-TAH-lee ar-kee-teht-TOH-nee-chee DEH-lee eh-dee-FEE-chee SO-no zbah-lor-DEE-tee-vee.]

47

REQUEST INFORMATION AT A TOURIST OFFICE

1. "Excuse me, can you provide some information about the city's attractions?" - "Scusi, può fornire informazioni sulle attrazioni della città?" [SKOO-zee, pwoh for-NEE-reh een-for-ma-tsyoh-nee SOO-leh aht-trah-TSYOH-nee DEHL-lah cheet-TAH?
2. "Where can I find a map of the city?" - "Dove posso trovare una mappa della città?" [DOH-veh POHs-soh tro-VAH-reh OO-nah MAH-pah DEL-lah cheet-TAH?]
3. "Are there any guided tours available?" - "Ci sono visite guidate disponibili?" [Chee SO-no VEE-zee-teh gwee-DAH-teh dee-spo-NEE-bee-lee?]
4. "What are the opening hours of the museums?" - "Quali sono gli orari di apertura dei musei?" [KWAH-lee SO-no gee oh-RAH-ree dee ah-PEHR-tu-rah DEE moo-ZEH-ee?]
5. "Can you recommend any local events or festivals happening during my visit?" - "Può consigliare qualche evento o festival locale che si svolge durante la mia visita?" [POO-oh kon-see-LYAH-reh KWAHL-keh eh-VEHN-toh oh fes-TEE-val lo-KAH-leh kee see SVOL-dje doo-RAN-teh lah MEE-ah vee-ZEE-tah?]
6. "Is there a tourist information center nearby?" - "C'è un centro informazioni turistiche nelle vicinanze?" [Cheh oon CHEN-tro een-for-ma-TSYOH-nee too-ree-STEE-keh NEHL-leh vee-chi-NAHN-tseh?]
7. "Do you have any brochures or pamphlets about the city's landmarks?" - "Ha dei volantini o opuscoli sulle attrazioni principali della città?" [Ah DEH-ee voh-lahn-TEE-nee oh oh-POOS-koh-lee SOO-leh aht-trah-TSYOH-nee preehn-chee-PAH-lee DEHL-lah cheet-TAH?]
8. "Can you provide information on public transportation options in the city?" - "Può fornire informazioni sulle opzioni di trasporto pubblico in città?" [POO-oh for-NEE-reh een-for-ma-tsyoh-nee SOO-leh ohp-TSYOH-nee dee trahs-POHR-toh POOB-blee-koh een cheet-TAH?]
9. "Are there any special discounts or offers for tourists?" - "Ci sono sconti o offerte speciali per i turisti?" [Chee SO-no SKOHN-tee oh oh-FER-teh speh-TSYAH-lee per ee too-REE-stee?]
10. "Is it possible to book guided tours or activities in advance?" - "È possibile prenotare visite guidate o attività in anticipo?" [EH poh-SEE-beh-leh pre-no-TAH-reh VEE-zee-teh gwee-DAH-teh oh aht-tee-VEE-tah een an-tee-CHEE-po?]

11

SHOPPING ITALIAN STYLE

Italy is considered one of the shopping capitals, hosting the world's most famous brands and highest class boutiques.

In particular, Milan is considered the fashion capital, but you will find something to suit you really everywhere, from north to south.

With the words and sentences in this chapter, you will be able to make questions about prices to requests for help, negotiatiate to payment, and tackle the experience of shopping in Italy with confidence and style.

Are you ready?

Let's begin our adventure into the world of Italian shopping!

COMMON SHOPPING WORDS

1. "Shop" - "Negozio" - [neh-GO-tsee-oh]
2. "Purchases" - "Acquisti" - [ah-KWEE-stee]
3. "Sale" - "Vendita" - [VEN-dee-tah]
4. "Discounts" - "Sconti" - [SKON-tee]

5. "Product" - "Prodotto" - [proh-DOT-toh]
6. "Price" - "Prezzo" - [PRET-tsoh]
7. "Payment" - "Pagamento" - [pah-gah-MEN-toh]
8. "Cash register" - "Cassa" - [KAHSS-sah]
9. "Shop window" - "Vetrina" - [veh-TREE-nah]
10. "Customer" - "Cliente" - [klee-EN-teh]
11. "Department" - "Reparto" - [reh-PAR-toh]
12. "Size" - "Taglia" - [TAHL-yah]
13. "Brand" - "Marca" - [MAR-kah]
14. "Clothing" - "Abbigliamento" - [ab-bee-lyah-MEN-toh]
15. "Shoes" - "Scarpe" - [SKAHR-peh]
16. "Bag" - "Borsa" - [BOR-sah]
17. "Offer" - "Offerta" - [of-FER-tah]
18. "Electronics" - "Elettronica" - [eh-leh-troh-NEE-kah]
19. "Coupon" - "Coupon" - [KOO-pohn]
20. "Return" - "Reso" - [REH-soh]
21. "Sales" - "Saldi" - [SAHL-dee]
22. "Discount" - "Sconto" - [SKOHN-toh]
23. "Purchases" - "Acquisti" - [ah-KWEE-stee]
24. "Shop window" - "Vetrina" - [veh-TREE-nah]
25. "Cash register" - "Cassa" - [KAH-ssah]
26. "Fitting" - "Prova" - [PROH-vah]
27. "Online store" - "Negozio online" - [neh-GO-tsee-oh on-LEEN]
28. "Clothing store" - "Negozio di abbigliamento" - [neh-GO-tsee-oh dee ab-bee-lyah-MEN-toh]
29. "Shopping mall" - "Centro commerciale" - [CHEN-tro kom-mehr-TCHA-leh]
30. "Department" - "Reparto" - [reh-PAR-toh]
31. "To buy" - "Comprare" - [kom-PRAH-reh]
32. "Payment" - "Pagamento" - [pah-gah-MEN-toh]
33. "Credit card" - "Carta di credito" - [KAHR-tah dee KREH-dee-toh]
34. "Cash" - "Contanti" - [kohn-TAHN-tee]
35. "Receipt" - "Scontrino" - [skohn-TREE-noh]
36. "Sale" - "Vendita" - [ven-DEE-tah]
37. "Return" - "Reso" - [REH-soh]
38. "Display" - "Esposizione" - [es-po-zee-TSYOH-neh]
39. "Fashion" - "Moda" - [MOH-dah]
40. "Offer" - "Offerta" - [oh-FEHR-tah]

INSIDE THE STORES

1. "How much does it cost?" - "Quanto costa?" [KWAHN-toh KO-sta?]
2. "Do you have this in a different size/color?" - "Hai questo in una taglia/colore diverso?" [AI KWEH-sto een OO-nah TAH-lyah/KO-loh-reh DEE-vehr-so?]
3. "Can I try it on?" - "Posso provarlo?" [POHS-so proh-VAHR-loh?]

50

4. "Is there a sale or any discounts available?" - "C'è uno sconto o qualche sconto disponibile?" [CHEH OO-no SKOHN-toh oh KWAL-keh SKOHN-toh dee-spo-NEE-bee-leh?]
5. "Can I pay by credit card?" - "Posso pagare con la carta di credito?" [POHS-so pah-GAH-reh kohn lah KAR-tah dee KREH-dee-toh?]
6. "Do you offer international shipping?" - "Offrite la spedizione internazionale?" [OH-FREE-teh lah speh-dee-TSYOH-neh een-tehr-nah-tsyoh-NAH-leh?]
7. "Can I get a receipt, please?" - "Posso avere una ricevuta, per favore?" [POHS-so ah-VEH-reh OO-nah ree-cheh-VOO-tah, pehr fah-VOH-reh?]
8. "Is there a warranty for this item?" - "C'è una garanzia per questo articolo?" [CHEH OO-nah gah-RAHN-tsya per DE-sto ar-TEE-koh-loh?]
9. "Where is the fitting room/changing room?" - "Dove si trova il camerino?" [DOH-veh see TROH-vah eel kah-meh-REE-no?]
10. "Do you have any recommendations for local shops or markets?" - "Avete delle raccomandazioni per negozi o mercati locali?" [AH-veh-teh DE-leh rah-koh-man-dah-tsyoh-nee per NEH-go-tsee oh mer-KAH-tee lo-KAH-lee?]

ASK PRICES AND SIZES

1. "How much does it cost?" - "Quanto costa?" [KWAHN-toh KOH-stah?]
2. "Is there a discount?" - "C'è uno sconto?" [CHEH OO-noh SCON-toh?]
3. "Do you have it in my size?" - "Ce l'hai nella mia taglia?" [CHEH LYEY-ee NEL-lah MEE-ah TAH-lyah?]
4. "What sizes do you have?" - "Quali taglie avete?" [KWAH-lee TAH-lyeh ah-VEH-teh?]
5. "Is this on sale?" - "È in saldo?" [EH een SAHL-doh?]
6. "Can I try it on?" - "Posso provarlo?" [POHs-soh proh-VAHR-loh?]
7. "Is there a different color available?" - "C'è un altro colore disponibile?" [CHEH oon AHL-troh koh-LOH-rey dee-SPO-nee-bee-leh?]
8. "Are there any special promotions?" - "Ci sono delle promozioni speciali?" [CHEE SOH-noh DEH-leh proh-moh-zee-OH-nee speh-chee-AH-lee?]
9. "What's the price range?" - "Qual è la fascia di prezzo?" [KWAH-leh lah FAH-syah dee PRET-soh?]
10. "Can I get a receipt, please?" - "Posso avere una ricevuta, per favore?" [POHs-soh ah-VEH-reh OO-nah ree-cheh-VOO-tah, pehr fah-VOH-reh?]

1. "Is the price negotiable?" - "Il prezzo è trattabile?" [EEL PRET-soh eh traht-TAH-bee-leh?]
2. "Can you give me a discount?" - "Puoi farmi uno sconto?" [PWAI FAHR-mee OO-noh SCON-toh?]
3. "What's the best price you can offer?" - "Qual è il miglior prezzo che puoi offrire?" [KWAHL EH eel mee-LYOR PRET-soh keh PWAI ohf-FEE-reh?]
4. "I'm interested in buying multiple items. Can we work out a better deal?" - "Sono interessato/a ad acquistare più articoli. Possiamo trovare un accordo migliore?" [SOH-noh in-teh-REHS-sah-toh/a ad ah-kwih-STAR-eh pew ahr-TEE-koh-lee. POHS-soh-moh troh-VAH-reh oon ahk-KOR-doh mee-LYOR-eh?]
5. "Is there a special discount for cash payments?" - "C'è uno sconto speciale per i pagamenti in contanti?" [CHEH OO-noh SCON-toh speh-chee-AH-leh per ee pah-gah-MEN-tee een kohn-TAHN-tee?]
6. "Can we meet halfway on the price?" - "Possiamo trovare un compromesso sul prezzo?" [POHS-soh-moh troh-VAH-reh oon kom-proh-MEH-soh sool PRET-soh?]
7. "Are there any ongoing promotions or bundle discounts?" - "Ci sono promozioni in corso o sconti per pacchetti?" [CHEE SO-noh proh-moh-TSEE-oh-nee een KOR-soh oh SCON-tee per pah-KET-tee?]
8. "I'm a regular customer. Can you offer me a loyalty discount?" - "Sono un cliente abituale. Puoi offrirmi uno sconto fedeltà?" [SOH-noh oon klee-EN-teh ah-bee-TWAH-leh. PWAI ohf-FEER-mee OO-noh SCON-toh feh-DEL-tah?]
9. "Is there a bulk discount for large orders?" - "C'è uno sconto per gli ordini di grandi quantità?" [CHEH OO-noh SCON-toh per lyee or-DEE-nee dee GRAHN-dee kwahn-TI-tah?]
10. "Can we negotiate the price if I buy other items as well?" - "Possiamo negoziare il prezzo se compro anche altri articoli?" [POHS-soh-moh neh-go-tsyah-reh eel PRET-soh seh KOM-proh AHN-keh AHL-tree-oh-lee?]

RETURNING OR EXCHANGING ITEMS

1. "Can I exchange it for a different size/color?" - "Posso cambiarlo con una taglia/un colore diverso?" [POH-soh kahm-BEE-ar-lo kohn OO-nah TAH-lyah/oohn koh-LOH-ray DEE-vehr-soh]
2. "The item is defective." - "L'articolo è difettoso." [LAR-tee-koh-loh eh dee-FET-toh-soh]
3. "Can I get a refund?" - "Posso avere un rimborso?" [POH-soh ah-VEH-ray oon reem-BOR-soh]
4. "I have the receipt." - "Ho lo scontrino." [OH loh scon-TREE-noh]

5. "The item was damaged during shipping." - "L'articolo è stato danneggiato durante la spedizione." [LAR-tee-koh-loh eh STAH-toh dahn-neh-GYA-toh doo-RAN-teh lah speh-dee-ZEE-oh-neh]
6. "Is there a return/exchange policy?" - "C'è una politica di reso/scambio?" [CHEH OO-nah poh-LEE-tee-kah dee RAY-soh/scahm-BEE-oh]
7. "I would like store credit instead of a refund." - "Vorrei un credito in negozio invece di un rimborso." [VOR-ay oon KREH-dee-toh een neh-GO-tsyoh een-VEH-chay dee oon reem-BOR-soh]
8. "Can I speak with a manager?" - "Posso parlare con un responsabile?" [POH-soh pahr-LAH-ray kohn oon rehs-POHN-sah-bee-lay]

THE ITALIAN NIGHT

When the sun sets, Italy comes alive with vibrant nightlife and unforgettable experiences.

This chapter is dedicated to assisting you in navigating the enthralling world of Italian nightlife and making the most of your evenings while in this enthralling country.

Whether you're hitting the trendy bars, dancing the night away in clubs, or indulging in delicious late-night meals, mastering the right phrases will enhance your nocturnal adventures.

From ordering drinks to mingling with locals, this chapter provides a comprehensive guide to express yourself with confidence and immerse yourself in the pulsating energy of Italy's nightlife scene.

Get ready for an unforgettable night out in the heart of Italy!

1. "Nightlife" - "Vita notturna" - [VEE-tah noht-TOON-nah]
2. "Bar" - "Bar" - [bar]

3. "Club" - "Club" - [kloob]
4. "Disco" - "Discoteca" - [dees-koh-TEH-kah]
5. "Pub" - "Pub" - [pub]
6. "Dance" - "Danza" - [DAN-tsah]
7. "Music" - "Musica" - [MOO-zee-kah]
8. "Party" - "Festa" - [FEH-stah]
9. "DJ" - "DJ" - [dee-jay]
10. "Live music" - "Musica dal vivo" - [MOO-zee-kah dal VEE-voh]
11. "Nightclub" - "Nightclub" - [nait-klab]
12. "Lounge" - "Lounge" - [launzh]
13. "Concert" - "Concerto" - [kon-CHER-toh]
14. "Drinks" - "Bevande" - [beh-VAN-deh]
15. "Dancing" - "Ballo" - [BAL-loh]
16. "Crowd" - "Folla" - [FOL-lah]
17. "Fun" - "Divertimento" - [dee-ver-tee-MEN-toh]
18. "Night out" - "Serata fuori" - [seh-RAH-tah FWOH-ree]
19. "Entertainment" - "Intrattenimento" - [een-trat-teh-NEE-men-toh]
20. "Socializing" - "Socializzare" - [soh-chee-ah-lee-TSah-reh]
21. "Clubbing" - "Clubbing" - [klahb-ing]
22. "Nightlife district" - "Quartiere della vita notturna" - [kwar-tee-EH-reh DEL-lah VEE-tah noht-TOON-nah]
23. "Live band" - "Band dal vivo" - [band dal VEE-voh]
24. "Karaoke" - "Karaoke" - [ka-rah-OH-keh]
25. "Late-night" - "Notte inoltrata" - [NOHT-tee ee-nol-TRAH-tah]
26. "Bar hopping" - "Giro dei bar" - [JEE-roh DEH-ee bar]
27. "Nighttime entertainment" - "Intrattenimento serale" - [een-trat-teh-NEE-men-toh seh-RAH-leh]
28. "Drinking" - "Bere" - [BEH-reh]
29. "Partygoer" - "Frequentatore di feste" - [freh-kwen-tah-TOH-reh dee FEH-steh]
30. "Night market" - "Mercato notturno" - [mer-KAH-toh noht-TOO-noh]
31. "Pub crawl" - "Giro dei pub" - [JEE-roh DEH-ee pub]
32. "Late-night snacks" - "Spuntini notturni" - [spoon-TEE-nee noht-TOON-ee]
33. "Dance floor" - "Pista da ballo" - [PEES-tah dah BAL-loh]
34. "Nighttime scenery" - "Paesaggio notturno" - [pah-eh-SAH-jo noht-TOO-noh]
35. "Nighttime tour" - "Tour notturno" - [toor noht-TOO-noh]
36. "Nighttime activities" - "Attività serali" - [aht-tee-VEE-tah seh-RAH-lee]
37. "Nightlife culture" - "Cultura della vita notturna" - [kul-TOO-rah DEL-lah VEE-tah noht-TOON-nah]
38. "Nighttime vibe" - "Vibrazione notturna" - [vee-brah-tsyoh-NEH noht-TOON-nah]
39. "Nighttime celebration" - "Celebrazione notturna" - [che-leh-brah-TSYOH-neh noht-TOON-nah]

40. "Nighttime adventure" - "Avventura notturna" - [ahv-ven-TOO-rah noht-TOON-nah]

INTERACTION AT THE BAR OR DISCO

1. "Can I have a cocktail, please?" - "Posso avere un cocktail, per favore?" [POHS-soh a-VEH-reh oon kohk-TEYL, per fa-VO- reh?]
2. "What's your most popular drink?" - "Qual è il tuo drink più popolare?" [KWAHL eh eel TOO-o drink pyoo po-po-LA-re?]
3. "Do you have any recommendations?" - "Hai qualche consiglio da darmi?" [AI KWAHL-keh kon-see-LYO dah DAR-mee?]
4. "Is there a cover charge?" - "C'è un costo d'ingresso?" [CHEH oon KOHS-toh deen-GRES-so?]
5. "Where's the dance floor?" - "Dov'è la pista da ballo?" [DOH-veh eh la PEE-sta dah BAL-lo?]
6. "Can I request a song?" - "Posso richiedere una canzone?" [POHS-so ree-kee-DEH-reh OO-nah kan-ZOH-neh?]
7. "Are there any special events tonight?" - "Ci sono eventi speciali stasera?" [CHEE SO-no e-VEHN-tee spe-tsyah-LEE sta-SEH-rah?]
8. "What time does the bar close?" - "A che ora chiude il bar?" [A keh OH-rah KYOO-deh eel bar?]
9. "Do you serve food here?" - "Si serve cibo qui?" [SEE SER-veh CHEE-bo kwee?]
10. "Cheers!" - "Salute!" [SA-LOO-teh!]

ASK ABOUT EVENTS AND PERFORMANCES

1. "Are there any live performances tonight?" - "Ci sono spettacoli dal vivo stasera?" [Chee SO-no speht-tah-KOH-lee dal VEE-vo stah-SEH-rah?]
2. "What kind of events do you have scheduled?" - "Che tipo di eventi avete in programma?" [Keh TEE-poh dee eh-VEHN-tee ah-VEH-teh een proh-GRAHM-mah?]
3. "Is there a DJ playing tonight?" - "C'è un DJ che suona stasera?" [Cheh oon DJ keh SWOH-nah stah-SEH-rah?]
4. "Are there any themed parties or special nights?" - "Ci sono feste a tema o serate speciali?" [Chee SO-no FEH-steh ah TEH-mah oh seh-RAH-teh speh-TSYA-lee?]
5. "Do I need to make a reservation for any upcoming events?" - "Devo prenotare per qualche evento imminente?" [DEH-vo preh-noh-TAH-reh per KWAHL-keh eh-VEHN-toh im-mee-NEN-teh?]
6. "Are there any discounts or promotions for tonight's events?" - "Ci sono sconti o promozioni per gli eventi di stasera?" [Chee SO-no SCON-tee oh proh-moh-TSYOH-nee per GLI eh-VEHN-tee dee stah-SEH- rah?]
7. "Can you tell me more about the live music lineup?" - "Puoi darmi più informazioni sulla scaletta di musica dal vivo?" [POO-oy DAHR-mee

pwee in-for-ma-TSYOH-nee SOO-lah ska-LET-tah dee MOO-zee-kah dal VEE-vo?]

8. "What time does the show start?" - "A che ora inizia lo spettacolo?" [Ah keh OH-rah in-EE-tsyah lo speh-ttah-KOH-lo?]
9. "Is there a dress code for the events?" - "C'è un dress code per gli eventi?" [Cheh oon dress code per gli eh-VEHN-tee?]
10. "Where can I find the event schedule?" - "Dove posso trovare il programma degli eventi?" [DOH-veh POHs-so troh-VAH-reh eel proh-GRAHM-mah deh-GLI eh-VEHN-tee?]

INVITING SOMEONE OUT

1. "Would you like to grab a coffee sometime?" - "Vuoi prendere un caffè insieme?" [VWOY prehn-DEH-reh oon kaf-FEH een-SEE-emeh?]
2. "Let's go out for dinner this weekend." - "Andiamo a cena questo weekend." [AHN-dee-ah-moh ah CHEH-nah KWEH-stoh weh-KEHND?]
3. "I heard there's a great concert next week. Want to go together?" - "Ho sentito che c'è un grande concerto la prossima settimana. Vuoi venire insieme?" [Oh sehn-TEE-toh keh cheh eh oon GRAHN-deh kohn-CHEHR-toh lah PROSS-ee-mah seht-TAH-nah. VWOY veh-NEE-reh een-SEE-emeh?]
4. "I'm planning to see a movie on Friday. Care to join me?" - "Ho in programma di vedere un film venerdì. Ti va di venire con me?" [Oh een proh-GRAHM-mah dee veh-DEH-reh oon feelm veh-NEHR-dee. Tee vah dee veh-NEE-reh kohn meh?]
5. "Let's explore the city together this weekend. Are you up for it?" - "Esploriamo la città insieme questo weekend. Sei interessato?" [Ehs-ploh-RYAH-moh lah CHEET-tah een-SEE-emeh KWEH-stoh weh-KEHND? Say in-TEH-ress-AH-toh?]
6. "There's a new art exhibition opening tomorrow. Would you like to check it out?" - "Domani inaugura una nuova mostra d'arte. Ti piacerebbe andare a vederla?" [Doh-MAH-nee een-OW-goo-rah OO-nah NOO-oh-vah MOHS-trah DAR-teh. Tee pyah-cheh-REB-beh ah ven-DEH-rah?]
7. "I'm going for a hike this Sunday. Want to join me and enjoy the outdoors?" - "Domani faccio un'escursione. Vuoi venire con me e goderti la natura?" [Doh-MAH-nee FAHT-cho oon-es-koor-SYO-neh. VWOY veh-NEE-reh kohn meh eh goh-DEHR-tee lah nah-TOO-rah?]
8. "There's a new restaurant in town. Let's try it out together." - "C'è un nuovo ristorante in città. Proviamolo insieme." [CHEH oon NOO-oh ree-stoh-RAHN-teh een CHEET-tah. Proh-VEE-ah-moh-loh een-SEE-emeh.]
9. "I'm planning a weekend getaway. Care to join me and escape the city?" - "Ho in programma una gita fuori porta nel weekend. Ti va di venire con me e scappare dalla città?" [Oh een proh-GRAHM-mah OO-nah GEE-

tah FWOH-ree POR-tah nel weh-KEHND. Tee vah dee veh-NEE-reh kohn meh eh skahp-PAH-reh DAHL-lah CHEET-tah?]

10. "Let's meet up for a drink after work. What do you say?" - "Incontriamoci per un drink dopo il lavoro. Che ne dici?" [Een-kohn-tree-AH-moh-chee per oon dreenk DOH-poh eel LAH-vo-roh. Keh neh DEE-chee?]

EXPRESSING MUSICAL PREFERENCES

1. "I love classical music. It's so soothing and elegant." - "Amo la musica classica. È così rilassante ed elegante." [AH-moh lah MOO-zee-kah KLAH-see-kah. Eh KOH-zee ree-lahs-SAHN-teh ed eh-leh-GAHN-teh.]

2. "I'm a big fan of rock music. The energy and rawness really resonate with me." - "Sono un grande fan della musica rock. L'energia e l'autenticità mi colpiscono davvero." [SO-no oon GRAHN-deh fahn DEHL-lah moo-ZEE-kah rohk. Leh-NEH-ree-gyah eh low-tehn-TEE-chee mee kol-PEE-skoh-no dahv-VEH-roh.]

3. "I enjoy listening to jazz. It's so improvisational and full of surprises." - "Mi piace ascoltare il jazz. È così improvvisativo e pieno di sorprese." [Mee pyah-cheh ahs-kohl-TAH-reh eel jahzz. Eh KOH-zee eem-prohv-vee-ZAH-tee-voh eh pyeh-noh dee sohr-PREH-zeh.]

4. "I'm really into pop music. It's catchy and great for dancing." - "Mi piace molto la musica pop. È orecchiabile e perfetta per ballare." [Mee pyah-cheh MOHL-toh lah moo-ZEE-kah pohp. Eh oh-rek-kee-AH-bee-leh eh pehr-FEHT-tah per bah-LAH-reh.]

5. "I'm a fan of electronic music. The beats and rhythms really get me moving." - "Sono un fan della musica elettronica. I ritmi e le basi mi fanno davvero ballare." [SO-no oon fahn DEHL-lah moo-ZEE-kah eh-leht-troh-NEE-kah. Ee REET-mee eh leh BAH-zee mee FAH-noh dahv-VEH-roh bah-LAH-reh.]

6. "I enjoy listening to country music. It has such heartfelt lyrics and tells stories." - "Mi piace ascoltare la musica country. Ha testi così sinceri e racconta storie." [Mee pyah-cheh ahs-kohl-TAH-reh lah moo-ZEE-kah KUHN-tree. Ah TES-tee KOH-zee seen-CHEH-ree eh rah-KOHN-tah STOH-ree-eh.]

7. "I'm really into hip-hop. The lyrics and flow are so impressive." - "Mi appassiona l'hip-hop. I testi e il flow sono davvero impressionanti." [Mee ahp-pahs-see-OH-nah leep-HOP. Ee TES-tee eh eel flow SOH-noh dahv-VEH-roh eem-prehss-see-OHN-tee.]

8. "I love listening to soul music. It's so soulful and full of emotion." - "Amo ascoltare la musica soul. È così profonda e piena di emozioni." [AH-moh ahs-kohl-TAH-reh lah moo-ZEE-kah sohl. Eh KOH-zee proh-FOHN-dah eh pyeh-nah dee eh-moh-TSYOH-nee.]

9. "I'm a big fan of indie rock. The unique sound and creativity really appeal to me." - "Sono un grande fan del rock indie. Il suono unico e la

creatività mi attraggono molto." [SO-no oon GRAHN-deh fahn dehl rohk in-DEE. Eel SWOH-noh OO-nee-koh eh lah kreh-ah-tee-VEE-tah mee aht-TRAH-goh-noh MOHL-toh.]

SAFETY PHRASES FOR THE NIGHT

1. "Excuse me, do you know the safest way to get back to my hotel from here?" - "Mi scusi, conosce la strada più sicura per tornare al mio hotel da qui?" [mee SKOO-zi, ko-NO-she la STRA-da pee-oo si-KU-ra per tor-NA-re al MIO o-tel da KWI?]
2. "Is it safe to walk alone at night in this area?" - "È sicuro camminare da soli di notte in questa zona?" [E si-KU-ro kam-mi-NA-re da SO-li di NOT-te in QUE-sta ZO-na?]
3. "Are there any areas I should avoid at night?" - "Ci sono zone che dovrei evitare di notte?" [chi SO-no ZO-ne ke DO-vrei e-vi-TA-re di NOT-te?]
4. "Could you recommend a reliable taxi service for late-night transportation?" - "Potrebbe consigliarmi un servizio di taxi affidabile per gli spostamenti notturni?" [po-TREB-be kon-si-LYAR-mi un ser-VI-zio di TA-ksi af-fi-DA-bi-le per gli spo-sta-MEN-ti not-TUR-ni?]
5. "I prefer to stay in well-lit and busy areas during the night." - "Preferisco stare in zone ben illuminate e frequentate durante la notte." [pre-fe-RI-sko STA-re in ZO-ne ben il-lu-mi-NA-te e fre-kwen-TA-te du-RAN-te la NOT-te]
6. "Is there a police station nearby? I need some assistance." - "C'è una stazione di polizia nelle vicinanze? Ho bisogno di assistenza." [che u-na sta-TSI-one di po-LI-tsi-a nel-le vi-ci-NAN-ze? O bi-SO-gno di as-si-STEN-za]
7. "Could you recommend a reputable night-time tour or activity in the area?" - "Potrebbe consigliarmi un tour o un'attività notturna affidabile nella zona?" [po-TREB-be kon-si-LYAR-mi un tour o un at-ti-VI-ta not-TUR-na af-fi-DA-bi-le NEL-la ZO-na]
8. "I'm feeling uncomfortable. Is there a well-populated area I can go to?" - "Mi sento a disagio. C'è una zona ben popolata in cui posso andare?" [mi SEN-to a di-SA-gio. che una ZO-na ben po-po-LA-ta in kwi POS-so an-DA-re?]
9. "What precautions should I take to ensure my safety during the night?" - "Quali precauzioni devo prendere per garantire la mia sicurezza durante la notte?" [KWAL-i pre-kau-TSION-i DE-vo pren-DE-re per gar-an-TI-re la mia si-KU-rez-za du-RAN-te la NOT-te]
10. "Excuse me, is this neighborhood considered safe after dark?" - "Mi scusi, questo quartiere è considerato sicuro dopo il tramonto?" [mee SKOO-zi, QUE-sto quar-TIE-re e kon-si-DE-ra-to si-KU-ro DO-po il tra-MON-to]

13

MUSEUMS AND GALLERIES

As we make our way through the museums and galleries in this chapter, we will set sail on an adventure that will take us into the realm of art, history, and culture.

Discover the wonders that lie within these cultural institutions and learn how to appreciate and engage with the artworks and exhibits on display.

Whether you're a seasoned art enthusiast or a curious traveler, this chapter will equip you with essential phrases to enhance your museum and gallery experience.

From asking for information to expressing your admiration, you'll gain the confidence to navigate these cultural spaces and delve deeper into the fascinating world of art.

Let's begin our cultural exploration!

WORDS RELATING TO ART AND CULTURE

1. "Art" - "Arte" - [AHR-teh]
2. "Culture" - "Cultura" - [kul-TOO-rah]
3. "Museum" - "Museo" - [moo-ZEH-oh]

4. "Exhibition" - "Mostra" - [MOH-strah]
5. "Gallery" - "Galleria" - [gahl-LEH-ree-ah]
6. "Painting" - "Pittura" - [pit-TOO-rah]
7. "Sculpture" - "Scultura" - [skool-TOO-rah]
8. "Architecture" - "Architettura" - [ar-kee-TEHT-too-rah]
9. "Music" - "Musica" - [MOO-zee-kah]
10. "Dance" - "Danza" - [DAHN-tsah]
11. "Theater" - "Teatro" - [teh-AH-troh]
12. "Literature" - "Letteratura" - [let-teh-rah-TOO-rah]
13. "Film" - "Film" - [FEELM]
14. "Photography" - "Fotografia" - [foh-toh-grah-FEE-ah]
15. "Poetry" - "Poesia" - [poh-eh-ZEE-ah]
16. "Cultural heritage" - "Patrimonio culturale" - [pa-tree-MOH-nee-oh kul-tur-AH-leh]
17. "Artistic expression" - "Espressione artistica" - [es-preh-SYOH-neh ar-tees-TEE-kah]
18. "Historical sites" - "Siti storici" - [SEE-tee stoh-REE-chee]
19. "Festival" - "Festival" - [feh-stee-VAHL]
20. "Artistic creativity" - "Creatività artistica" - [kreh-ah-tee-VEE-tah ar-tees-TEE-kah]

TALKING ABOUT ART

1. "The brushstrokes in this painting are exquisite." - "Le pennellate in questo dipinto sono squisite." [leh pehn-neh-LAH-teh in KWEH-sto di-PEEN-toh SO-no skwee-ZEE-teh]
2. "The sculpture captures the essence of human emotion" - "La scultura cattura l'essenza dell'emozione umana." [la skool-TOO-rah kah-TOO-rah less-EN-za dell eh-moh-tsee-OH-ne oo-MAH-na]
3. "The artist's use of light and shadow creates a dramatic effect" - "L'uso della luce e dell'ombra da parte dell'artista crea un effetto drammatico." [LOO-soh DEL-la LOO-cheh e del-LOMB-rah da PAR-teh del-lar-TEE-sta KRE-ah oon eh-FEHT-toh dram-MAH-tee-koh]
4. "This artwork reflects the artist's unique perspective" - "Quest'opera d'arte riflette la prospettiva unica dell'artista." [kweh-STOH-peh-rah dar-teh rif-LET-teh la pro-speh-TEE-va OO-nee-ca del-LAR-tee-sta]
5. "The composition of this photograph is visually striking" - "La composizione di questa fotografia è visivamente sorprendente." [la kom-po-zee-TSEE-oh-neh di KWE-sta foto-GRA-fee-ah eh vee-zoo-AH-men-te sor-PREN-den-teh]
6. "The museum showcases a diverse collection of contemporary art." - "Il museo espone una collezione diversificata di arte contemporanea." [il moo-ZAY-oh es-POH-neh OOH-na ko-LEH-see-oh-neh dee-ver-see-fee-KAH-tah di AR-teh kon-tem-poh-RAH-ne-ah]
7. "This sculpture embodies the spirit of Renaissance art." - "Questa scultura incarna lo spirito dell'arte rinascimentale." [KWE-sta skool-

61

TOO-rah in-CAR-na lo spee-REE-to del-LAR-teh ree-nah-shee-men-TAH-leh]

8. "The gallery features an impressive array of abstract paintings." - "La galleria presenta un'impressionante varietà di dipinti astratti." [la gal-LEH-ree-ah preh-SEN-tah oon-im-preh-see-OHN-te va-ree-eh-TAH di di-PIN-ti as-TRAT-ti]

9. "The artwork depicts a poignant moment in history." - "L'opera d'arte raffigura un momento commovente della storia." [LO-peh-rah dar-teh raf-fee-GOO-rah oon mo-MEN-to kom-mo-VENT-te DEL-la STO-ree-ah]

10. "The exhibit highlights the cultural heritage of the region." - "La mostra mette in evidenza il patrimonio culturale della regione." [la MOH-strah MET-te in eh-vee-DEN-tza il pa-tree-MOH-nee-oh kool-too-RAH-leh DEL-la reh-JOH-neh]

ASKING FOR INFORMATION ABOUT WORKS OF ART

1. "Can you provide some background information on this painting?" - "Puoi fornire alcune informazioni di base su questo dipinto?" [pwoy for-NEE-reh ahl-KOO-neh een-fohr-MA-tsee-OH-nee dee BA-seh soo KWEH-stoh dee-PEEN-toh]

2. "What is the significance of this sculpture in the art world?" - "Qual è il significato di questa scultura nel mondo dell'arte?" [kwal eh eel see-nee-fee-KAH-toh dee kwe-stah skool-TOO-rah nel MOHN-doh del-LAR-teh]

3. "Could you tell me the inspiration behind this artwork?" - "Potresti dirmi l'ispirazione dietro a questa opera d'arte?" [poh-TRES-tee DEER-mee lees-pee-rah-TSEE-oh-neh DEE-eht-roh a kwe-stah OH-peh-rah DAR-teh]

4. "I'm curious about the artist's creative process for this piece." - "Sono curioso del processo creativo dell'artista per questa opera." [SO-noh koo-ree-OH-zoh del pro-CHESS-oh kreh-AH-tee-voh del-LAR-teest-ah per kwe-STAH OH-peh-rah]

5. "Is there a particular meaning or symbolism associated with this installation?" - "C'è un significato o simbolismo particolare associato a questa installazione?" [cheh oon see-nee-fee-KAH-toh oh see-mbo-LEES-moh par-tee-KOH-leh a-so-see-AH-toh ah kwe-STAH een-stahl-lah-tsee-OH-neh]

6. "Can you explain the historical context of this artifact?" - "Puoi spiegare il contesto storico di questo manufatto?" [pwoy spee-EH-gah-reh eel kon-TEH-stoh stoh-REE-koh dee kwe-STOH mah-noo-FAHT-toh]

7. "What materials were used to create this sculpture?" - "Quali materiali sono stati utilizzati per creare questa scultura?" [KWAH-lee mah-teh-ree-ah-lee SOH-noh STAH-tee oo-tee-lee-TSAT-tee per kreh-AH-reh kwe-STAH skool-TOO-rah]

8. "Are there any interesting stories or anecdotes related to this artwork?" - "Ci sono storie o aneddoti interessanti legati a questa opera d'arte?" [chee SO-noh STOH-ree-eh oh ah-nehd-DOH-tee een-ter-es-SAHN-tee leh-GAH-tee ah kwe-STAH OH-peh-rah DAR-teh]

9. "Could you recommend any other works by the same artist?" - "Potresti consigliare altre opere dello stesso artista?" [poh-TRES-tee kohn-see-LYAH-reh AHL-treh OH-peh-reh DEL-LOH STES-so ar-TEES-tah]

10. "Is there a guide or audio tour available for this exhibition?" - "C'è una guida o un tour audio disponibile per questa mostra?" [cheh OO-nah GWEE-dah oh oon toor AW-dee-oh dee-spo-NEE-bee-leh per kwe-STAH MOH-strah]

DIALOGUING WITH A TOUR GUIDE

1. "Can you tell us more about the historical background of this site?" - "Puoi raccontarci di più sul contesto storico di questo luogo?" [pwoy ra-kon-TAR-kee dee PEE-sool soo-KON-tes-toh STOH-ree-koh dee KWEH-stoh LOO-oh-go]

2. "What are some interesting facts or stories associated with this landmark?" - "Quali sono alcuni fatti interessanti o storie legate a questo punto di riferimento?" [KWAH-lee SO-noh AHL-koo-nee FAT-tee een-ter-es-SAN-tee oh STOH-ree-eh leh-GAH-teh ah KWEH-stoh POON-toh dee ree-feh-REE-men-toh]

3. "Could you explain the architectural style of this building?" - "Potresti spiegare lo stile architettonico di questo edificio?" [poh-TRES-tee spee-EH-gah-reh loh STEE-leh ar-kee-teht-TOH-nee-koh dee KWEH-stoh eh-DEE-fee-tsee-oh]

4. "Are there any special events or exhibitions happening at this museum?" - "Ci sono eventi o mostre speciali in corso in questo museo?" [chee SO-noh eh-VENT-ee oh MO-streh speh-TSYAH-lee een KOR-soh een KWEH-stoh moo-ZEH-oh]

5. "Can you recommend any other must-see attractions in the area?" - "Puoi consigliare altre attrazioni da non perdere nella zona?" [pwoy kon-see-LYAH-reh AHL-treh aht-tra-TSYOH-nee dah non per-DEH-reh nel-LAH ZOH-nah]

6. "What is the significance of the artwork displayed in this gallery?" - "Qual è il significato delle opere d'arte esposte in questa galleria?" [KWAHL eh eel see-nee-fee-KAH-toh DEHL-leh ZOH-reh DAR-teh es-PO-steh een KWEH-stah ga-LEHR-ree-ah]

7. "Are there any specific guidelines or rules visitors should be aware of while exploring the museum?" - "Ci sono linee guida o regole specifiche che i visitatori dovrebbero conoscere durante l'esplorazione del museo?" [chee SO-noh LEE-neh GWEE-dah oh REH-goh-leh speh-SEE-kee kee ee vee-see-TAH-toh-ree do-vrehb-beh-roh nohn-osh-KEH-reh doo-RAN-teh lehs-ploh-rah-TSYOH-neh del moo-ZEH-oh]

63

8. "Can you share some interesting anecdotes or stories related to the artifacts on display?" - "Puoi condividere qualche aneddoto o storia interessante legata agli artefatti in mostra?" [pwoy kon-dee-VEE-reh KWAH-leh ah-neh-DOH-toh oh STOH-ree-ah een-ter-es-SAHN-teh leh-GAH-tah ahrt-teh-FAHT-tee een MO-strah]

9. "Is there a particular tour or theme that you would recommend for a more in-depth experience?" - "C'è un tour o un tema particolare che consiglieresti per un'esperienza più approfondita?" [cheh oon toor oh oon TEH-mah par-tee-KOH-leh kee kon-see-LYEH-res-tee per oon-es-peh-ree-EHN-tsah pju a-pro-FON-dee-tah]

10. "How long would you recommend spending in this museum to fully appreciate its collection?" - "Quanto tempo consiglieresti di dedicare a questo museo per apprezzare appieno la sua collezione?" [KWAHN-toh TEHM-po kon-see-LYEH-res-tee dee deh-dee-KAH-reh a KWEH-stoh moo-ZEH-oh per ap-prez-ZAH-reh ah-PYEH-noh lah SOO-ah kol-LEHT-see-OH-neh]

EXPRESS OPINIONS ABOUT ART AND CULTURE

1. "I find this artwork to be truly captivating." - "Trovo questa opera d'arte davvero affascinante." [TRO-vo KWEH-sta OH-peh-rah DAR-teh dav-VEH-ro af-fa-shee-NAN-te]

2. "In my opinion, this sculpture represents raw emotion." - "Secondo me, questa scultura rappresenta emozioni autentiche." [se-KON-do meh, KWEH-sta skool-TOO-rah rap-pre-SEN-ta eh-mo-TSYOH-nee ow-ten-TEE-keh]

3. "The use of colors in this painting is quite impressive." - "L'utilizzo dei colori in questo dipinto è davvero impressionante." [loo-TEE-zzo dei KO-loh-ree een KWEH-sto dee-PIN-toh eh dav-VEH-ro im-pres-syo-NAN-te]

4. "I'm really drawn to the abstract nature of this piece." - "Sono davvero attratto dalla natura astratta di questo pezzo." [SO-no dav-VEH-ro at-TRAHT-to dah-LAH nah-TOO-rah as-TRAT-tah dee KWEH-sto PETS-so]

5. "This exhibit showcases a beautiful blend of traditional and contemporary art." - "Questa esposizione mette in mostra un bellissimo mix di arte tradizionale e contemporanea." [KWEH-sta es-po-ZEE-tsyoh-neh MET-te een MOH-stah oon bel-LEES-see-mo meeks dee AR-te tra-dee-tsyoh-NA-leh e con-tem-poh-ra-NAY-a]

6. "The attention to detail in this artwork is remarkable." - "L'attenzione per i dettagli in questa opera d'arte è notevole." [la-ten-TSYOH-neh per ee DET-ta-ly een KWEH-sta OH-peh-rah DAR-teh eh no-TEH-vo-leh]

7. "I appreciate the artist's unique perspective on this subject matter." - "Apprezzo la prospettiva unica dell'artista su questo argomento." [a-PRET-tso la pros-pe-TTY-va OO-nee-ka del-LAR-tees-ta soo KWEH-sto ar-go-MEN-to]

8. "The symbolism in this piece is thought-provoking." - "Il simbolismo in questo pezzo fa riflettere." [eel sim-BO-lees-mo een KWEH-sto PETTS-so fa rif-let-TEH-re]

9. "This sculpture evokes a sense of tranquility and serenity." - "Questa scultura evoca una sensazione di tranquillità e serenità." [KWEH-sta skool-TOO-rah eh-VO-ka OO-na sen-za-TSYOH-neh dee trahn-kwee-LEE-ta e seh-reh-NEE-ta]

10. "The composition of this photograph is visually striking." - "La composizione di questa fotografia è visivamente sorprendente." [la kom-po-see-TSYOH-neh dee KWEH-sta fo-to-GRA-fee-ah eh vee-zoo-al-MEN-te sor-pren-DEN-te]

REQUESTING ASSISTANCE AT A MUSEUM

1. "Excuse me, could you provide some information about this artwork?" - "Mi scusi, potrebbe fornirmi delle informazioni su questa opera d'arte?" [mee SKOO-zee, po-TREB-be for-NEER-mee DEH-le in-for-ma-TSYOH-nee soo KWEH-sta OH-peh-rah DAR-teh?]

2. "Is there a guided tour available for this exhibition?" - "È disponibile una visita guidata per questa mostra?" [eh dees-po-NEE-bee-le OO-na vee-ZEE-ta gwee-DA-ta per KWEH-sta MOH-stra?]

3. "Could you recommend any must-see pieces in this museum?" - "Potrebbe consigliarmi qualche opera imperdibile in questo museo?" [po-TREB-bee kon-see-LYAR-mee KWAL-keh OH-peh-rah eem-per-DEE-bee-le een KWEH-sto moo-ZAY-o?]

4. "I'm having trouble understanding the context of this painting. Could you offer some insight?" - "Ho difficoltà a comprendere il contesto di questo dipinto. Potrebbe darmi qualche spiegazione?" [oh dee-fee-KOHL-ta a kom-pren-DEH-re eel kohn-TESS-to dee KWEH-sto dee-PIN-toh. po-TREB-be dar-mee KWAL-keh spee-ga-TSYOH- neh?]

5. "Are there any audio guides or brochures available to enhance the museum experience?" - "Ci sono guide audio o brochure disponibili per arricchire l'esperienza museale?" [che SO-no GWE-deh OW-dee-oh o bro-SHOO-re dee-spo-NEE-bee-lee per ar-REEK-kee-reh leh-speh-ree-EN-za moo-ZAY-A-le?]

6. "I'm interested in learning more about the historical background of this exhibit. Is there any additional information I can access?" - "Sono interessato a saperne di più sul contesto storico di questa esposizione. È possibile accedere a ulteriori informazioni?" [SO-no een-ter-ESS-a-to a sa-PEHR-neh dee pee SOOL kohn-TESS-to STOR-ee-ko dee KWEH-sta es-po-ZEE-tsyoh-neh. eh po-SEE-bee-le at-CHEH-deh-reh a oo-lee-teh-REE in-for-ma-TSYOH- nee?]

7. "Can you direct me to the nearest restroom?" - "Mi può indicare dov'è il bagno più vicino?" [mee pwo een-dee-KA-reh doh-VEH eel BAHN-yo pyoo vee-CHEE-no?]

8. "Are photography or video recordings allowed in this museum?" - "È permesso fotografare o registrare video in questo museo?" [eh per-MES-so fo-to-gra-FAH-re o re-jee-STRAR-re vee-DEE-o een KWEH-sto moo-ZAY-o?]

9. "Is there a coat check service available for visitors?" - "È disponibile un servizio di guardaroba per i visitatori?" [eh dee-SPO-nee-bee-le oon ser-VEE-tsyoh dee goo-ar-DAH-ro-ba per ee vee-zee-TA-to-ree?]

10. "I seem to have misplaced my audio guide. Is there a way to replace it or get a new one?" - "Sembra che abbia perso la mia guida audio. È possibile sostituirla o ottenerne una nuova?" [SEM-bra keh AB-bya PER-so la MEE-a GWEE-da OW-dee-oh. eh po-SEE-bee-le sos-tee-TEER-la o ot-teh-NER-neh OO-na NOO-va?]

14

RELAXATION AND LEISURE TIME

This chapter takes a deep dive into the world of leisure and relaxation, studying terms that may help enrich your experience of the Italian "dolce vita." These phrases can allow you thoroughly immerse yourself in the Italian way of life, whether you are resting at the beach, wandering through lovely streets, or enjoying a leisurely lunch at a charming café.

From expressing preferences and interests to planning activities and seeking recommendations, this chapter is your guide to making the most of your leisure time in Italy.

Get ready to unwind, indulge, and embrace the true essence of la dolce vita.

COMMON LEISURE WORDS

1. "Festival" - "Festival" - [feh-stee-VAHL]
2. "Vacanza" - "Vacation" - [vah-KAN-tsa]
3. "Spiaggia" - "Beach" - [spyahd-jah]
4. "Spa" - "Spa" - [spah]

5. "Amaca" - "Hammock" - [ah-MAH-kah]
6. "Ritiro" - "Retreat" - [ree-TEE-roh]
7. "Relax" - "Relaxation" - [ree-LAHKS]
8. "Tranquillità" - "Tranquility" - [trahn-kwee-LEE-tah]
9. "Serenità" - "Serenity" - [seh-reh-NEE-tah]
10. "Meditazione" - "Meditation" - [meh-dee-tah-TSYOH-neh]
11. "Yoga" - "Yoga" - [YOH-gah]
12. "Massaggio" - "Massage" - [mahs-SAH-joh]
13. "Natura" - "Nature" - [nah-TOO-rah]
14. "Escursionismo" - "Hiking" - [eh-skoo-zee-oh-NEES-moh]
15. "Picnic" - "Picnic" - [PEE-kneek]
16. "Tempo libero" - "Leisure" - [TEM-poh lee-BEH-roh]
17. "Rilassante" - "Relaxing" - [ree-lah-SAHN-teh]
18. "Rilassarsi" - "Unwind" - [ree-lah-SAR-see]
19. "Gioia" - "Joy" - [JOH-yah]
20. "Ricreazione" - "Recreation" - [ree-kreh-ah-TSYOH-neh]

SENTENCES FOR BEACHES AND PARKS

1. "The beach is very crowded today." - "La spiaggia è molto affollata oggi." [lah spee-AH-jah eh MOHL-toh ah-fohl-LAH-tah OH-jee]
2. "Where is the nearest park?" - "Dove si trova il parco più vicino?" [DOH-veh see TROH-vah eel PAHR-koh pyoo vee-CHEE-noh]
3. "Let's go for a swim." - "Andiamo a fare un bagno." [ahn-DYAH-moh ah FAH-reh oon BAH-nyoh]
4. "Can we have a picnic in the park?" - "Possiamo fare un picnic nel parco?" [pohs-SYAH-moh FAH-reh oon PEE-nik nel PAHR-koh]
5. "Don't forget your sunscreen." - "Non dimenticare la tua crema solare." [non dee-men-tee-KAH-reh lah TOO-ah KREH-mah soh-LAH-reh]
6. "The sea is very calm today." - "Il mare è molto calmo oggi." [eel MAH-reh eh MOHL-toh KAL-moh OH-jee]
7. "I love to watch the sunset at the beach." - "Amo guardare il tramonto sulla spiaggia." [AH-moh gwahr-DAH-reh eel trah-MON-toh SOO-lah spee-AH-jah]
8. "The park is open until sunset." - "Il parco è aperto fino al tramonto." [eel PAHR-koh eh ah-PEHR-toh FEE-noh al trah-MON-toh]
9. "We can play volleyball at the beach." - "Possiamo giocare a pallavolo in spiaggia." [pohs-SYAH-moh joh-KAH-reh ah pah-la-VOH-loh een spee-AH-jah]
10. "The kids are playing in the park." - "I bambini stanno giocando nel parco." [ee BAHM-bee-nee STAH-noh joh-KAHN-doh nel PAHR-koh]
11. "There are many beautiful shells on the beach." - "Ci sono molte belle conchiglie sulla spiaggia." [chee SOH-noh MOHL-teh BEHL-leh kon-KEE-lyeh SOO-lah spee-AH-jah]

12. "We should bring a parasol to the beach." - "Dovremmo portare un parasole in spiaggia." [doh-VRAY-moh pohr-TAH-reh oon PAH-rah-soh-leh een spee-AH-jah]
13. "Let's rent a paddle boat." - "Affittiamo un pedalò." [ahf-fee-TYAH-moh oon peh-dah-LOH]
14. "The park has many walking trails." - "Il parco ha molti sentieri per camminare." [eel PAHR-koh ah MOHL-tee sen-TYAY-ree pehr kam-mee-NAH-reh]
15. "Watch out for the jellyfish." - "Attento alle meduse." [ah-TEN-toh AHL-leh meh-DOO-seh]
16. "The park is a great place for a barbecue." - "Il parco è un ottimo posto per un barbecue." [eel PAHR-koh eh oon OH-tee-moh POH-stoh pehr oon bar-beh-KOO]
17. "Remember to bring a towel." - "Ricorda di portare un asciugamano." [ree-KOHR-dah dee pohr-TAH-reh oon ah-shoo-gah-MAH-noh]
18. "The beach has a lifeguard." - "La spiaggia ha un bagnino." [lah spee-AH-jah ah oon BAH-nyee-noh]
19. "The park is a perfect spot for reading." - "Il parco è un posto perfetto per leggere." [eel PAHR-koh eh oon POH-stoh PEHR-feht-toh pehr leh-JEH-reh]
20. "Don't forget to clean up before leaving the beach." - "Non dimenticare di pulire prima di lasciare la spiaggia." [non dee-men-tee-KAH-reh dee poo-LEE-reh PREE-mah dee lah-SHAH-reh lah spee-AH-jah]

BOOKING SPA OR WELLNESS TREATMENTS

1. "I would like to book a massage." - "Vorrei prenotare un massaggio." [voh-RAY preh-no-TAH-reh oon mahs-SAH-jo]
2. "Do you have any appointments available on Saturday?" - "Avete qualche appuntamento disponibile sabato?" [AH-veh-teh KWAL-keh ah-poon-tah-MEN-toh dees-pon-EE-bee-leh sah-BAH-toh]
3. "What types of treatments do you offer?" - "Quali tipi di trattamenti offrite?" [KWAH-lee TEE-pee dee trah-tah-MEN-tee ohf-FREE-teh]
4. "I'm interested in a facial treatment." - "Sono interessato a un trattamento facciale." [SOH-noh een-teh-rehs-SAH-toh ah oon trah-tah-MEN-toh fah-CHAH-leh]
5. "Can I use the spa facilities after my treatment?" - "Posso usare le strutture della spa dopo il mio trattamento?" [POH-soh OO-zah-reh leh stroo-TOO-reh DEL-lah spa DOH-poh eel MEE-oh trah-tah-MEN-toh]
6. "Do you offer couple's treatments?" - "Offrite trattamenti di coppia?" [ohf-FREE-teh trah-tah-MEN-tee dee KOH-pee-ah]
7. "How long does the treatment take?" - "Quanto tempo dura il trattamento?" [KWAN-toh TEHM-poh DOO-rah eel trah-tah-MEN-toh]

8. "What's included in the wellness package?" - "Cosa è incluso nel pacchetto benessere?" [KOH-zah eh een-KLOO-zoh nel PAH-ket-toh beh-NEH-seh-reh]

9. "I need to cancel my appointment." - "Ho bisogno di cancellare il mio appuntamento." [OH bee-ZOH-nyoh dee kan-chell-AH-reh eel MEE-oh ah-poon-tah-MEN-toh]

10. "Can I reschedule my appointment to next week?" - "Posso riprogrammare il mio appuntamento per la prossima settimana?" [POH-soh ree-proh-grahm-MAH-reh eel MEE-oh ah-poon-tah-MEN-toh pehr lah PROHS-see-mah seh-tee-MAH-nah]

SPORTS CENTER AND GOLF COURSE

1. "Can I rent a golf cart?" - "Posso noleggiare un carrello da golf?" [POH-soh noh-LEH-jah-reh oon kah-REL-loh dah golf]

2. "I'd like to book a tee time." - "Vorrei prenotare un orario di partenza." [voh-RAY preh-no-TAH-reh oon oh-RAH-ryo dee pahr-TEN-zah]

3. "Do you offer golf lessons?" - "Offrite lezioni di golf?" [ohf-FREE-teh leh-TSYOH-nee dee golf]

4. "Where's the first hole?" - "Dove si trova il primo buco?" [DOH-veh see TROH-vah eel PREE-moh BOO-koh]

5. "What's my handicap?" - "Qual è il mio handicap?" [KWAHL eh eel MEE-oh han-dee-KAP]

6. "I'd like to buy some golf balls." - "Vorrei comprare delle palline da golf." [voh-RAY kom-PRAH-reh DEL-leh pah-LEE-neh dah golf]

7. "Can I book the driving range?" - "Posso prenotare il campo di pratica?" [POH-soh preh-no-TAH-reh eel KAHM-poh dee PRAH-tee-kah]

8. "Where is the clubhouse?" - "Dove si trova il clubhouse?" [DOH-veh see TROH-vah eel CLUB-howse]

9. "I would like to participate in the tournament." - "Vorrei partecipare al torneo." [voh-RAY par-teh-chee-PAH-reh al tor-NAY-oh]

10. "Can you recommend a golf instructor?" - "Puoi consigliare un istruttore di golf?" [pwoh-EE kon-see-LYAH-reh oon ees-TROO-toh-reh dee golf]

EXPRESSING YOUR EMOTIONS WHILE RELAXING

1. "I feel very relaxed." - "Mi sento molto rilassato." [mee SEN-toh MOHL-toh ree-LAH-sah-toh]

2. "This place is so calming." - "Questo posto è così tranquillizzante." [KWEH-stoh POH-stoh eh koh-ZEE trahn-kwee-lee-ZAHN-teh]

3. "I'm enjoying this peaceful moment." - "Sto godendo di questo momento di pace." [STOH go-DEHN-doh dee KWEH-stoh mo-MEN-toh dee PAH-cheh]

4. "This is just what I needed to unwind." - "È proprio quello di cui avevo bisogno per rilassarmi." [eh PROH-pryo KWEL-loh dee koo-ee ah-VEH-voh bee-ZOH-nyoh pehr ree-LAH-sahr-mee]
5. "I love the serene atmosphere here." - "Amo l'atmosfera serena qui." [AH-moh laht-moh-SFEH-rah seh-REH-nah KEE]
6. "The sound of the waves is so soothing." - "Il suono delle onde è così rilassante." [eel soo-OH-noh DEL-leh ON-deh eh koh-ZEE ree-LAH-sahn-teh]
7. "I feel so much lighter after that massage." - "Mi sento così più leggero dopo quel massaggio." [mee SEN-toh koh-ZEE pyoo leh-JEH-roh DOH-poh KWEHL mahs-SAH-jo]
8. "The aroma of the essential oils is very calming." - "L'aroma degli oli essenziali è molto calmante." [L'AH-roh-mah DEH-lee OH-lee es-sen-TSYAH-lee eh MOHL-toh kal-MAN-teh]
9. "Meditation helps me to relax." - "La meditazione mi aiuta a rilassarmi." [lah meh-dee-tah-TSYOH-neh mee ah-YOO-tah ah ree-LAH- sahr-mee]
10. "I feel so at ease in this environment." - "Mi sento così a mio agio in questo ambiente." [mee SEN-toh koh-ZEE ah MEE-oh AH-joh in KWEH-stoh ahm-BYEN-teh]

15

COOKING AND FOOD PREPARATION

The varied flavors and long-standing culinary traditions of Italian food have earned it a well-deserved reputation the world over.

In this chapter, we will delve into the art of Italian cooking and examine words that will assist you in confidently navigating the kitchen.

Your experience in the kitchen will be more enjoyable if you grasp the terminology used in food preparation, regardless of whether you are a novice or an expert cook.

From mastering essential cooking techniques to understanding ingredient names and measurements, this chapter will equip you with the necessary vocabulary and phrases to create authentic Italian dishes.

Get ready to immerse yourself in the delicious world of Italian gastronomy and bring the flavors of Italy into your own kitchen.

KITCHEN-SPECIFIC VOCABULARY

1. "Recreation" - "Ricreazione" - [ree-kreh-ah-TSYOH-neh]

2. "Food" - "Cibo" - [CHEE-boh]
3. "Kitchen" - "Cucina" - [koo-CHEE-nah]
4. "Chef" - "Chef" - [shef]
5. "Recipe" - "Ricetta" - [ree-CHEHT-tah]
6. "Dishes" - "Piatti" - [pee-AHT-tee]
7. "Preparation" - "Preparazione" - [preh-pah-rah-TSYOH-neh]
8. "Ingredients" - "Ingredienti" - [een-greh-DYEN-tee]
9. "Cutting board" - "Tagliere" - [tah-LYEH-reh]
10. "Stove" - "Fornello" - [for-NEL-loh]
11. "Refrigerator" - "Frigorifero" - [free-goh-REE-feh-roh]
12. "Pot" - "Pentola" - [pen-TOH-lah]
13. "Pan" - "Padella" - [pah-DEL-lah]
14. "Ladle" - "Mestolo" - [mes-TOH-loh]
15. "Knife" - "Coltello" - [kol-TEL-loh]
16. "Fork" - "Forchetta" - [for-KET-tah]
17. "Spoon" - "Cucchiaio" - [kook-KYAH-yoh]
18. "Glass" - "Bicchiere" - [beek-KYEH-reh]
19. "Cup" - "Tazza" - [TAHT-tsah]
20. "Oven" - "Forno" - [FOR-noh]
21. "Microwave" - "Microonde" - [mee-kroh-OHN-deh]
22. "Blender" - "Frullatore" - [frool-lah-TOH-reh]
23. "Juicer" - "Spremiagrumi" - [spreh-mee-ah-GROO-mee]
24. "Grater" - "Grattugia" - [graht-TOO-jah]
25. "Mandolin" - "Mandrino" - [mahn-DREE-noh]
26. "Coffee machine" - "Macchina per il caffè" - [mahk-KEE-nah per eel KAH-feh]
27. "Sieve" - "Setaccio" - [seh-TAHT-tsyoh]
28. "Mold" - "Muffa" - [MOOF-fah]
29. "Risotto" - "Risotto" - [ree-SOT-toh]
30. "Tart" - "Crostata" - [kroh-STAH-tah]
31. "Squeezing" - "Spremitura" - [spreh-mee-TOO-rah]
32. "Slicer" - "Affettatrice" - [af-fet-TAH-tree-cheh]
33. "Cooking" - "Cucinare" - [koo-chee-NAH-reh]
34. "Dough" - "Impasto" - [im-PAH-stoh]
35. "Frying" - "Friggere" - [frij-JEH-reh]
36. "Grilling" - "Grigliare" - [gri-LYAH-reh]
37. "Stirring" - "Mescolare" - [mes-ko-LAH-reh]
38. "Seasoning" - "Condimento" - [kon-dee-MEN-toh]
39. "Sauce" - "Salsa" - [SAL-sah]
40. "Baking" - "Panificazione" - [pa-nee-fee-kah-TSYOH-neh]
41. "Marinating" - "Marinare" - [mah-ree-NAH-reh]
42. "Portioning" - "Porzionare" - [por-tsyoh-NAH-reh]
43. "Sorbet" - "Sorbetto" - [sor-BET-toh]
44. "Dusting" - "Spolverare" - [spol-ve-RAH-reh]
45. "Syrup" - "Sciroppo" - [shee-ROHP-poh]
46. "Garnishing" - "Guarnire" - [gwar-NEE-reh]

47. "Stew" - "Stufato" - [stoo-FAH-toh]
48. "Frittata" - "Frittata" - [frit-TAH-tah]
49. "Pan-frying" - "Friggere in padella" - [frij-JEH-reh in pah-DEL-lah]
50. "Traditional cuisine" - "Cucina tradizionale" - [koo-CHEE-nah tra-dee-tsyoh-NAH-leh]

FOLLOWING A RECIPE

1. "Let's start with gathering all the ingredients." - "Iniziamo raccogliendo tutti gli ingredienti." [ee-nee-TSYAH-moh rah-KOH-jen-doh TOOT-tee lyee in-greh-DYEN-tee]
2. "Preheat the oven to 180 degrees." - "Preriscalda il forno a 180 gradi." [pre-ree-SKAL-dah eel FOR-noh ah CHEN-toh-TOH-tah GRAH-dee]
3. "Chop the vegetables into small pieces." - "Taglia le verdure a pezzetti." [TAH-lyah leh ver-DOO-reh ah pez-ZEH-tee]
4. "Stir the mixture until it's smooth." - "Mescola il composto fino a quando non è liscio." [meh-SKOH-lah eel kohm-POH-stoh FEE-noh ah KWAN-doh non eh LEES-kyoh]
5. "Let the dough rise for two hours." - "Lascia lievitare l'impasto per due ore." [LAH-shah lee-eh-vee-TAH-reh leem-PAH-stoh pehr DOO-eh OH-reh]
6. "Pour the batter into the baking pan." - "Versa l'impasto nella teglia da forno." [VEHR-sah leem-PAH-stoh nel-lah TEH-lyah dah FOR-noh]
7. "Cook on low heat for 30 minutes." - "Cucina a fuoco basso per 30 minuti." [koo-CHEE-nah ah FOO-koh BAH-soh pehr TREHN-tah MEE-noo-tee]
8. "Season the meat with salt and pepper." - "Condire la carne con sale e pepe." [kohn-DEE-reh lah KAR-neh kohn SAH-leh eh PEH-peh]
9. "Chill the dessert in the fridge before serving." - "Raffredda il dolce nel frigo prima di servire." [rahf-FREH-dah eel DOHL-cheh nel FREE-goh PREE-mah dee sehr-VEER-eh]
10. "Add the tomatoes to the sautéed onions." - "Aggiungi i pomodori alle cipolle saltate." [ah-JOON-jee ee poh-MOH-doh-ree AHL-leh chee-POHL-leh sahl-TAH-teh]
11. "Blend until you have a creamy consistency." - "Frulla fino a ottenere una consistenza cremosa." [FROO-llah FEE-noh ah ot-teh-NEH-reh oon-ah koh-sis-TEN-tsah kreh-MOH-zah]
12. "Follow the steps in the recipe." - "Segui i passaggi nella ricetta." [seh-GOO-ee ee pah-SAH-jee NEL-lah ree-CHEH-tah]
13. "Let the soup simmer for 15 minutes." - "Lascia sobbollire la zuppa per 15 minuti." [LAH-shah soh-bohl-LEER-eh lah ZOOP-pah pehr KWEEN-dee-chee MEE-noo-tee]
14. "Sift the flour before adding it." - "Setaccia la farina prima di aggiungerla." [seh-TAH-chah lah fah-REE-nah PREE-mah dee ah-joon-GEHR-lah]

74

15. "Use fresh ingredients for the best flavor." - "Usa ingredienti freschi per il miglior sapore." [OO-sah in-greh-DYEN-tee FREH-skee pehr eel MEE-jor sah-POH-reh]
16. "Stir occasionally to prevent sticking." - "Mescola occasionalmente per evitare che si attacchi." [meh-SKOH-lah oh-kah-zee-oh-nahl-MEN-teh pehr eh-VAH-reh keh see ah-TAH-kee]
17. "Let the cake cool before icing it." - "Lascia raffreddare la torta prima di glassarla." [LAH-shah rahf-FREH-dah-reh lah TOR-tah PREE-mah dee glah-SAR-lah]
18. "This recipe serves four people." - "Questa ricetta serve per quattro persone." [KWEH-stah ree-CHEH-tah SEHR-veh pehr KWAT-troh pehr-SOH-neh]
19. "Grate the cheese over the pasta." - "Grattugia il formaggio sulla pasta." [grat-TOO-jah eel for-MAH-joh SOO-lah PAH-stah]
20. "Bake until golden brown." - "Cuoci fino a doratura." [koo-OH-chee FEE-noh ah doh-ra-TOO-rah]

ASK FOR ADVICE ON WINES AND PAIRINGS

1. "What wine would you recommend with this dish?" - "Quale vino consiglierebbe con questo piatto?" [KWAH-leh VEE-noh kon-see-LYAH-reh-beh kohn KWEH-stoh PYAH-toh]
2. "Do you have a wine that pairs well with fish?" - "Avete un vino che si abbina bene al pesce?" [ah-VEH-teh oon VEE-noh keh see ah-BEE-nah BEH-neh al PEH-sheh]
3. "I prefer a dry wine." - "Preferisco un vino secco." [preh-feh-REE-sko oon VEE-noh SEK-koh]
4. "Do you think a red or white wine would be better with the cheese?" - "Pensi che un vino rosso o bianco sarebbe meglio con il formaggio?" [PEN-see keh oon VEE-noh ROS-soh oh BYAHN-koh sah-REHB-beh MEH-lyoh kohn eel for-MAH-joh]
5. "I would like to try a local wine." - "Vorrei provare un vino locale." [vor-REH-ee pro-VAH-reh oon VEE-noh lo-KAH-leh]
6. "Can I see the wine list?" - "Posso vedere la carta dei vini?" [POS-soh veh-DEH-reh lah KAR-tah dei VEE-nee]
7. "We would like a bottle of your best red wine." - "Vorremmo una bottiglia del vostro miglior vino rosso." [vor-REH-moh oon-ah boh-TEE-lyah del VOS-troh me-JOR VEE-noh ROS-soh]
8. "I enjoy full-bodied wines." - "Mi piacciono i vini corposi." [mee PYAH-tsyoh-noh ee VEE-nee kor-POH-see]
9. "What's a good wine to go with the dessert?" - "Quale è un buon vino da abbinare al dolce?" [KWAH-leh eh oon bwohn VEE-noh dah ah-bee-NAH-reh al DOHL-cheh]
10. "Is this a sweet or dry wine?" - "È questo un vino dolce o secco?" [EH KWEH-sto oon VEE-noh DOHL-cheh oh SEK-koh]

16

ITALIAN DESSERTS

Italian desserts are not just a delicious indulgence; they represent a rich legacy of regional and seasonal traditions, recipes handed down from generation to generation, and flavorful, fresh local ingredients. From North to South, each region of Italy boasts its own specialty, from simple, rustic desserts to complex, refined creations.

In our journey through the panorama of Italian desserts, we will encounter classics such as tiramisu, the irresistible spoon dessert made with ladyfinger cookies, mascarpone and coffee, and panna cotta, a creamy, velvety dessert that melts in your mouth. But there will also be room for lesser-known but equally delicious regional desserts, such as the Neapolitan pastiera, an Easter cake rich with wheat, ricotta and candied fruit, or the Sicilian cannolo, a fried dough cylinder filled with a rich ricotta cream.

If you are ready to dive into this sweet journey, then let's go - "Onward to dessert!"

1. "Dessert" - "Dolce" - [DOHL-che]
2. "Ice Cream" - "Gelato" - [jeh-LAH-toh]
3. "Cake" - "Torta" - [TOHR-tah]
4. "Pie" - "Torta" - [TOHR-tah]
5. "Pastry" - "Pasticceria" - [pahs-TEETCH-eh-ree-ah]
6. "Custard" - "Crema" - [KREH-mah]
7. "Cream" - "Panna" - [PAHN-nah]
8. "Sugar" - "Zucchero" - [TSOO-kheh-ro]
9. "Chocolate" - "Cioccolato" - [cho-koh-LAH-toh]
10. "Candy" - "Caramella" - [kar-ah-MEH-lah]
11. "Biscuit" - "Biscotto" - [bees-KOH-toh]
12. "Honey" - "Miele" - [MYEH-leh]
13. "Jam" - "Marmellata" - [mar-meh-LAH-tah]
14. "Pudding" - "Budino" - [boo-DEE-noh]
15. "Muffin" - "Muffin" - [MOO-ffin]
16. "Cupcake" - "Cupcake" - [KOOP-kehk]
17. "Donut" - "Ciambella" - [cham-BEH-lah]
18. "Tiramisu" - "Tiramisù" - [tee-rah-mee-SOO]
19. "Cannoli" - "Cannoli" - [kan-NOH-lee]
20. "Fruit" - "Frutta" - [FROOT-tah]
21. "Berries" - "Bacche" - [BAK-keh]
22. "Almond" - "Mandorla" - [man-DOR-lah]
23. "Hazelnut" - "Nocciola" - [noh-CHOH-lah]
24. "Walnut" - "Noce" - [NOH-che]
25. "Coconut" - "Cocco" - [KOH-koh]
26. "Pistachio" - "Pistacchio" - [pis-TAHK-kio]
27. "Cinnamon" - "Cannella" - [kan-NEL-lah]
28. "Cheesecake" - "Cheesecake" - [CHEEZ-kehk]
29. "Macaron" - "Macaron" - [MAK-a-ron]
30. "Caramel" - "Caramello" - [ka-ra-MEH-lo]
31. "Vanilla" - "Vaniglia" - [va-NEE-lya]
32. "Sponge Cake" - "Pan di Spagna" - [pan dee SPAN-ya]
33. "Meringue" - "Meringa" - [me-REEN-gah]
34. "Pancake" - "Pancake" - [PAN-kehk]
35. "Waffle" - "Waffle" - [WAHF-fehl]
36. "Shortbread" - "Biscotto di pasta frolla" - [bees-KOH-toh dee PAH-stah FROH-llah]
37. "Butter" - "Burro" - [BOOR-roh]
38. "Cream Puff" - "Bignè" - [been-YEH]
39. "Panna Cotta" - "Panna Cotta" - [PAHN-nah KOH-tah]
40. "Strudel" - "Strudel" - [STROO-del]

1. "Could I have a slice of cake, please?" - "Potrei avere una fetta di torta, per favore?" [POH-trey ah-VEH-reh OOH-nah FEHT-tah dee TOHR-tah, pehr fah-VOH-reh]

2. "I would like to order the chocolate mousse." - "Vorrei ordinare la mousse al cioccolato." [Voh-REH-ee or-dee-NAH-reh lah MOOS-seh al choh-koh-LAH-toh]

3. "What is the dessert of the day?" - "Qual è il dolce del giorno?" [Kwahl EH eel DOHL-che del JOHR-noh]

4. "Do you have any sugar-free desserts?" - "Avete dei dolci senza zucchero?" [AH-veh-teh day DOHL-chee SEHN-zah TSOO-kheh-roh]

5. "I'll have the tiramisu, please." - "Prenderò il tiramisù, per favore." [Prehn-DEH-roh eel tee-rah-mee-SOO, pehr fah-VOH-reh]

6. "Could I see the dessert menu?" - "Potrei vedere il menù dei dolci?" [POH-trey veh-DEH-reh eel meh-NOO day DOHL-chee]

7. "Does this dessert contain nuts?" - "Questo dolce contiene noci?" [KWEH-stoh DOHL-che kohn-TYEH-neh NOH-chee]

8. "Can I have a coffee with the dessert?" - "Posso avere un caffè con il dolce?" [POH-soh ah-VEH-reh oon kah-FEH kohn eel DOHL-che]

9. "Is this pastry gluten-free?" - "Questa pasticceria è senza glutine?" [KWEH-stah pahs-TEETCH-eh-ree-ah EH SEHN-zah gloo-TEE-neh]

10. "I would like some ice cream, please." - "Vorrei del gelato, per favore." [Voh-REH-ee del jeh-LAH-toh, pehr fah-VOH-reh]

11. "Could I have this dessert to take away?" - "Potrei avere questo dolce da portare via?" [POH-trey ah-VEH-reh KWEH-stoh DOHL-che dah pohr-TAH-reh VEE-ah]

12. "What is in this pastry?" - "Cosa c'è in questa pasticceria?" [KOH-sah cheh in KWEH-stah pahs-TEETCH-eh-ree-ah]

13. "Could I get some whipped cream on the side?" - "Potrei avere della panna montata a parte?" [POH-trey ah-VEH-reh DEL-lah PAHN-nah mon-TAH-tah ah PAR-teh]

14. "Can I try a sample of that gelato?" - "Posso provare un assaggio di quel gelato?" [POH-soh pro-VAH-reh oon ah-SAHJ-yoh dee KWEHL jeh-LAH-toh]

15. "How big are the portions?" - "Quanto sono grandi le porzioni?" [KWAN-toh SOH-noh GRAHN-dee leh por-TSYOH-nee]

16. "Do you have any vegan desserts?" - "Avete dei dolci vegani?" [AH-veh-teh day DOHL-chee veh-GAH-nee]

17. "I'd like to order the cheesecake." - "Vorrei ordinare la cheesecake." [Voh-REH-ee or-dee-NAH-reh la CHEEZ-kehk]

18. "Is this dessert dairy-free?" - "Questo dolce è senza latticini?" [KWEH-stoh DOHL-che eh SEHN-zah lah-tee-CHEE-nee]

19. "Do you have any fruit tarts?" - "Avete delle crostate di frutta?" [AH-veh-teh DEL-leh kroh-STA-teh dee FROOT-tah]

20. "Could I get the dessert with less sugar?" - "Potrei avere il dolce con meno zucchero?" [POH-trey ah-VEH-reh eel DOHL-che kohn MEH-noh TSOO-kheh-roh]

17

BEACH AND SEA TIME

Let's move the sun-kissed shores of Italy, where the beach becomes a playground of relaxation and fun.

In this chapter, we dive into the world of beach culture and equip you with essential phrases to make the most of your seaside adventures.

Whether you're lounging under an umbrella, splashing in the crystal-clear waters, or indulging in beachside delicacies, speaking the language of the beach will enhance your experience and connect you with the vibrant coastal atmosphere.

From asking for directions to ordering refreshing drinks, we've got you covered. Get ready to soak up the sun, feel the sand between your toes, and embrace the beauty of the Italian coast.

VOCABULARY FOR THE SEA AND THE BEACH

1. "Beach" - "Spiaggia" - [spee-AH-jah]
2. "Sand" - "Sabbia" - [SAHB-byah]

3. "Sea" - "Mare" - [MAH-reh]
4. "Wave" - "Onda" - [OHN-dah]
5. "Sun" - "Sole" - [SOH-leh]
6. "Beach umbrella" - "Ombrellone" - [om-brel-LOH-neh]
7. "Towel" - "Asciugamano" - [ah-shoo-gah-MAH-noh]
8. "Swimsuit" - "Costume da bagno" - [koh-STOO-meh dah BAH-nyoh]
9. "Pool" - "Piscina" - [pee-SHEE-nah]
10. "Sun lounger" - "Sdraio" - [SDRAH-yoh]
11. "Palm tree" - "Palma" - [PAHL-mah]
12. "Seashell" - "Conchiglia" - [kon-KEE-lyah]
13. "Sandcastle" - "Castello di sabbia" - [kah-STEHL-loh dee SAHB-byah]
14. "Sunscreen" - "Crema solare" - [KREH-mah soh-LAH-reh]
15. "Seawater" - "Acqua di mare" - [AHK-kwah dee MAH-reh]
16. "Surfing" - "Surf" - [serf]
17. "Snorkeling" - "Snorkeling" - [snor-KEH-ling]
18. "Wind" - "Vento" - [VEN-toh]
19. "Boat" - "Barca" - [BAHR-kah]
20. "Relaxation" - "Relax" - [reh-LAHKS]

RESERVING A SUNBED OR UMBRELLA

1. "I would like to book a beach umbrella, please." - "Vorrei prenotare un ombrellone, per favore." [vor-REH-ee preh-no-TAH-reh oon ohm-breh-LOH-neh, pehr fah-VOH-reh]
2. "Do you have any beach umbrellas available for this weekend?" - "Avete ombrelloni disponibili per questo weekend?" [ah-VEH-teh ohm-breh-LOH-nee dees-poh-NEE-bee-lee pehr KWEH-stoh WEE-kend]
3. "What is the price for a beach umbrella rental?" - "Qual è il prezzo per il noleggio di un ombrellone?" [kwal EH eel PRET-tsoh pehr eel noh-LEH-joh dee oon ohm-breh-LOH-neh]
4. "Could we reserve an umbrella close to the water?" - "Potremmo riservare un ombrellone vicino all'acqua?" [po-TREHM-moh ree-sehr-VAH-reh oon ohm-breh-LOH-neh vee-CHEE-noh ahl-AHK-wah]
5. "How many beach chairs come with the umbrella?" - "Quante sdraio vengono con l'ombrellone?" [KWAN-teh SDRAH-yoh VEN-goh-noh kohn l'ohm-breh-LOH-neh]
6. "I need a beach umbrella for two people." - "Ho bisogno di un ombrellone per due persone." [oh bee-ZOH-nyoh dee oon ohm-breh-LOH-neh pehr doo-eh pehr-SOH-neh]
7. "Can I book the umbrella for the whole week?" - "Posso prenotare l'ombrellone per tutta la settimana?" [POHS-soh preh-no-TAH-reh l'ohm-breh-LOH-neh pehr TOOT-tah lah seh-tee-MAH-nah]
8. "Is the beach umbrella included in the hotel reservation?" - "L'ombrellone è incluso nella prenotazione dell'hotel?" [l'ohm-breh-LOH-neh EH een-KLOO-soh neh-lah preh-no-tah-TSYOH-neh del-LOH-tehl]

9. "I would like to cancel my beach umbrella reservation." - "Vorrei cancellare la mia prenotazione dell'ombrellone." [vor-REH-ee kan-cheh-LAH-reh lah MEE-ah preh-no-tah-TSYOH-neh del-LOH-tehl]
10. "Do we need to bring our own beach towels, or are they provided with the umbrella?" - "Dobbiamo portare i nostri asciugamani da spiaggia o sono forniti con l'ombrellone?" [DOH-bbyah-moh por-TAH-reh ee NOS-tree ah-shoo-gah-MAH-nee dah spee-AH-jah oh SOH-noh for-NEE-tee kohn l'ohm-breh-LOH-neh]

AT KIOSK OR BEACH BAR

1. "Could I have the menu, please?" - "Potrei avere il menu, per favore?" [POH-trey ah-VEH-reh eel meh-NOO, pehr fah-VOH-reh]
2. "Do you serve food here?" - "Servite cibo qui?" [ser-VEE-teh CHEE-boh KWE]
3. "I would like a cold drink." - "Vorrei una bevanda fredda." [vor-REH-ee OO-nah bev-AN-dah FREH-dah]
4. "Can I order a cocktail?" - "Posso ordinare un cocktail?" [POS-soh or-dee-NAH-reh oon cohk-TAYL]
5. "Do you have any specials today?" - "Avete qualche offerta speciale oggi?" [ah-VEH-teh KWAL-keh ohf-FER-tah speh-TSYAH-leh OH-jee]
6. "Could I get a beer, please?" - "Potrei avere una birra, per favore?" [POH-trey ah-VEH-reh OO-nah BEER-rah, pehr fah-VOH-reh]
7. "Where can I find the restrooms?" - "Dove posso trovare i servizi igienici?" [DOH-veh POS-soh tro-VAH-reh ee ser-VEE-tsyee ee-JEE-eh-nee-chee]
8. "What time do you close?" - "A che ora chiudete?" [ah keh OR-ah kyoo-DEH-teh]
9. "Could I have the check, please?" - "Potrei avere il conto, per favore?" [POH-trey ah-VEH-reh eel KON-toh, pehr fah-VOH-reh]
10. "Is there a table available?" - "C'è un tavolo disponibile?" [cheh oon tah-VOH-loh dees-poh-NEE-bee-leh]

EXPRESS CLIMATIC CONDITIONS

1. "It's hot today." - "Fa caldo oggi." [fa KAL-do OD-djee]
2. "The weather is beautiful." - "Il tempo è bellissimo." [eel TEM-po eh bel-LIS-see-mo]
3. "It's raining." - "Sta piovendo." [sta pee-o-VEN-do]
4. "The sun is shining." - "Il sole sta splendendo." [eel SO-le sta splen-DEN-do]
5. "It's windy outside." - "Fuori c'è vento." [foo-OH-ree CHE ven-to]
6. "The sky is clear." - "Il cielo è sereno." [eel CHEE-e-lo eh se-RE-no]
7. "It's foggy this morning." - "C'è nebbia stamattina." [CHE NEB-bia sta-mat-TEE-na]

8. "It's snowing heavily." - "Sta nevicando abbondantemente." [sta ne-vee-CAN-do ab-bon-dan-TE-men-te]
9. "There's a thunderstorm coming." - "Sta arrivando un temporale." [sta arri-VAN-do oon tem-po-RA-le]
10. "The temperature is dropping." - "La temperatura sta scendendo." [la tem-pe-ra-TU-ra sta SHEN-den-do]

CALL FOR ASSISTANCE OR RESCUE ON THE BEACH

1. "Could you help me, please?" - "Potrebbe aiutarmi, per favore?" [po-TREHB-beh ahyoo-TAR-mee, per fah-VOH-reh]
2. "I think I'm having a sunstroke." - "Credo di avere un colpo di sole." [KREH-doh dee ah-VEH-reh oon COL-po di SOH-leh]
3. "I can't find my children." - "Non riesco a trovare i miei bambini." [non RYEH-scoh a tro-VAH-reh ee MYEH-ee bam-BEE-nee]
4. "I lost my bag, can you help me?" - "Ho perso la mia borsa, puoi aiutarmi?" [oh PEHR-soh la MEE-ah BOR-sah, PWOH-ee ahyoo-TAR-mee]
5. "Could you call a lifeguard?" - "Potresti chiamare un bagnino?" [po-TREH-stee kyah-MAH-reh oon ban-YEE-noh]
6. "I need a doctor." - "Ho bisogno di un medico." [oh bee-ZOH-nyoh dee oon MEH-dee-koh]
7. "Do you have a first aid kit?" - "Avete un kit di primo soccorso?" [ah-VEH-teh oon kit di PREE-moh SOH-kor-soh]
8. "I got stung by a jellyfish." - "Sono stato puntato da una medusa." [SOH-noh STA-toh poon-TAH-toh dah OO-nah meh-DOO-sah]
9. "Could you help me apply sunscreen?" - "Potresti aiutarmi a mettere la crema solare?" [po-TREH-stee ahyoo-TAR-mee a meh-TEH-reh la KREH-mah so-LAH-reh]
10. "I can't swim, can you help me get to the shore?" - "Non so nuotare, puoi aiutarmi a raggiungere la riva?" [non soh nwah-TAH-reh, pwoh-ee ahyoo-TAR-mee a rah-JOON-ge-reh la REE-vah]

18

ROMANCE AND THE PERFECT DATE

Italy, with its breathtaking scenery, vibrant culture, and ardent people, serves as the ideal setting for love and romance.

Whether you're on a romantic getaway or looking to impress someone special, mastering the art of expressing love in Italian will add an extra touch of charm to your experience.

In this chapter, we will explore a collection of phrases that will help you convey your feelings, plan the perfect date, and create unforgettable romantic moments.

From sweet compliments to heartfelt declarations, this guide will empower you to express your love in the language of amore.

Get ready to ignite the flames of passion and create lifelong memories in the most romantic country in the world.

WORDS ABOUT LOVE

1. "Love" - "Amore" - [ah-MOH-reh]

2. "Romance" - "Romanticismo" - [roh-man-TEE-seez-moh]
3. "Passion" - "Passione" - [pahs-see-OH-neh]
4. "Heart" - "Cuore" - [KWOH-reh]
5. "Affection" - "Affetto" - [ah-FEHT-toh]
6. "Desire" - "Desiderio" - [deh-zee-DEH-ree-oh]
7. "Devotion" - "Devozione" - [deh-voh-TSYOH-neh]
8. "Attraction" - "Attrazione" - [aht-trah-TSYOH-neh]
9. "Intimacy" - "Intimità" - [een-tee-MEE-tah]
10. "Kiss" - "Bacio" - [BAH-cho]
11. "Hug" - "Abbraccio" - [ahb-BRAH-chyo]
12. "Cuddle" - "Coccola" - [koh-KOH-lah]
13. "Companion" - "Compagno/Compagna" - [kom-PAH-nyoh/kom-PAH-nyah]
14. "Soulmate" - "Anima gemella" - [AH-nee-mah jeh-MEL-lah]
15. "Romantic" - "Romantico/Romantica" - [roh-MAN-tee-koh/roh-MAN-tee-kah]
16. "Date" - "Appuntamento" - [ah-poon-tah-MEN-toh]
17. "Marriage" - "Matrimonio" - [mah-tree-MOH-nyoh]
18. "Relationship" - "Relazione" - [reh-lah-TSYOH-neh]
19. "Commitment" - "Impegno" - [eem-PEH-nyoh]
20. "Eternal" - "Eterno/Eterna" - [eh-TEHR-noh/eh-TEHR-nah]

EXPRESS AFFECTION AND FEELINGS

1. "I love you." - "Ti amo." [tee AH-moh]
2. "You are beautiful." - "Sei bellissima/o." [say bel-LEE-see-mah/oh]
3. "You make me happy." - "Mi fai felice." [mee fai feh-LEE-cheh]
4. "I adore you." - "Ti adoro." [tee ah-DOH-roh]
5. "You are my sunshine." - "Sei il mio sole." [say eel MEE-oh SOH-leh]
6. "I miss you." - "Mi manchi." [mee MAHN-kee]
7. "You mean the world to me." - "Significhi il mondo per me." [see-nee-fee-kee eel MOHN-doh pehr mee]
8. "You are my everything." - "Sei tutto per me." [say TOO-toh pehr mee]
9. "You have a special place in my heart." - "Hai un posto speciale nel mio cuore." [hai oon POH-stoh speh-chee-AH-leh nel MEE-oh KWOH-reh]
10. "I am grateful to have you in my life." - "Sono grato/a di averti nella mia vita." [SOH-no GRAH-toh/ah dee ah-VEHR-tee nel-LAH MEE-ah VEE-tah]

I hope these phrases will help you express your affection and feelings in Italian!

PHRASES FOR INVITING SOMEONE OUT

1. "Would you like to go out for dinner with me?" - "Ti va di uscire a cena con me?" [tee va di u-SHE-re a CHE-na con me?]

2. "Let's grab a coffee together." - "Andiamo a prendere un caffè insieme." [an-DYA-mo a pren-DE-re un caf-FE in-SYE-me]
3. "I would love to take you to the movies." - "Mi piacerebbe portarti al cinema." [mi pia-che-REB-be por-TAR-ti al chi-NE-ma]
4. "How about going for a walk in the park?" - "Cosa ne dici di fare una passeggiata al parco?" [KO-sa ne DI-chi di FA-re una pas-se-GIA-ta al PAR-co]
5. "Let's go out for drinks and have a good time." - "Usciamo a prendere qualcosa e divertiamoci." [u-SHA-mo a pren-DE-re qual-CO-sa e di-ver-TYA-mo-chi]
6. "I have tickets to a concert. Would you like to come with me?" - "Ho dei biglietti per un concerto. Ti piacerebbe venire con me?" [o dei bi-LYET-ti per un con-CER-to. ti pia-che-REB-be VE-ni-re con me]
7. "Let's explore the city together this weekend." - "Esploriamo la città insieme questo weekend." [es-plo-RIA-mo la CHIT-ta in-SYE-me QUE-sto WE-kend]
8. "I know a great restaurant. Shall we go there for dinner?" - "Conosco un ottimo ristorante. Andiamo lì a cena?" [co-NOS-co un OT-ti-mo ri-sto-RAN-te. an-DYA-mo LI a CHE-na?]
9. "There's a new art exhibition. Would you be interested in going?" - "C'è una nuova mostra d'arte. Saresti interessato/a a venire?" [CE una NO-va MO-stra D'AR-te. sa-RES-ti in-te-res-SA-to/a a VE-ni-re?]
10. "I'm planning a day trip to the countryside. Would you like to join me?" - "Sto pianificando una gita in campagna. Vorresti venire con me?" [sto pia-ni-FI-can-do una GI-ta in cam-PA-nya. vor-RES-ti VE-ni-re con me?]

DIALOGUES DURING A ROMANTIC DINNER

1. "The candlelight creates a romantic ambiance." - "La luce delle candele crea un'atmosfera romantica." [La loo-cheh DEH-lay kan-DEH-leh KREH-a oon-a-tohs-fera ro-man-TEE-cah.]
2. "The food tastes even better when shared with you." - "Il cibo ha un sapore ancora migliore quando lo condivido con te." [Eel CHEE-boh ah oon sah-POH-reh an-KOH-rah MEEL-yoh-reh KWAHN-doh lo kon-DEE-vee-doh kon teh.]
3. "Your presence makes this dinner truly special." - "La tua presenza rende questa cena veramente speciale." [La TOO-ah pre-SEN-tza REN-deh KWE-sta CHEH-nah veh-rah-MEN-teh spe-chee-AH-leh.]
4. "I'm grateful for this moment with you." - "Sono grato/a per questo momento con te." [SO-no GRA-toh/GRA-tah per KWE-sto mo-MEN-to kon teh.]
5. "Every bite is a delight." - "Ogni boccone è un piacere." [OH-nyee bo-KOH-neh eh oon pya-CHE-reh.]

6. "The wine perfectly complements the flavors." - "Il vino si abbina perfettamente ai sapori." [Eel VEE-no see ahb-BEE-nah per-feh-TAH-men-teh ahee sah-POH-ree.]
7. "Your smile is the most beautiful thing I've ever seen." - "Il tuo sorriso è la cosa più bella che abbia mai visto." [Eel TOO-oh sor-REE-zoh eh la KO-sah pyoo BEL-la keh AHB-bya MAI VEES-to.]
8. "Let's make a toast to our love and happiness." - "Facciamo un brindisi al nostro amore e alla nostra felicità." [FAH-tcha-mo oon breen-DEE-zee al NO-stro a-MOH-reh eh AHL-la NO-strah feh-lee-CHEE-ta.]
9. "This dinner feels like a dream come true." - "Questa cena sembra un sogno diventato realtà." [KWE-sta CHEH-nah SEM-bra oon SOG-no dee-VEN-ta-to ree-ahl-TAH.]
10. "Thank you for making this evening unforgettable." - "Grazie per aver reso questa serata indimenticabile." [GRA-tsyeh per ah-VER REH-so KWE-sta se-RAH-ta in-dee-men-tee-CAH-beh-leh.]

PROPOSE A TOAST

1. "Let's raise our glasses and toast to love and happiness." - "Alziamo i nostri bicchieri e brindiamo all'amore e alla felicità." [al-TSYA-mo ee NO-stree beek-KYE-ree eh breen-DEE-amoh ahl-la-MOH-reh eh AHL-la feh-lee-CHEE-tah.]
2. "Here's to a lifetime of beautiful moments together." - "Brindiamo a una vita di momenti meravigliosi insieme." [breen-DEE-ah-moh ah OO-nah VEE-tah dee moh-MEN-tee meh-rah-VEE-glee-oh-see een-SYE-meh.]
3. "Cheers to the future and all the adventures it holds." - "Salute al futuro e a tutte le avventure che ci riserva." [sa-LOO-teh al fuh-TOO-roh eh ah TOOT-teh leh ahv-ven-TOO-reh keh chee REE-zehr-vah.]
4. "Let's make a toast to our love and the beautiful memories we've created." - "Facciamo un brindisi al nostro amore e ai bellissimi ricordi che abbiamo creato." [FAH-cha-moh oon breen-DEE-zee al NO-stro a-MOH-reh eh ah-ee bel-lee-SEE-mee ree-KOR-dee keh ahb-BYA-moh kree-AH-toh.]
5. "Here's to a bright and promising future together." - "Brindiamo a un futuro luminoso e promettente insieme." [breen-DEE-ah-moh ah oon foo-TOO-roh loo-mee-NOH-so eh proh-met-TEN-teh een-SYE-meh.]
6. "Cheers to love, laughter, and a lifetime of cherished moments." - "Salute all'amore, alle risate e a una vita di momenti preziosi." [sa-LOO-teh al-LAH-moh-reh, AL-le ree-SA-teh eh ah OO-nah VEE-tah dee moh-MEN-tee preh-ZYO-zee.]
7. "Let's raise a glass to the joy and happiness we bring to each other's lives." - "Alziamo un bicchiere alla gioia e alla felicità che portiamo nelle nostre vite reciproche." [al-TSYA-moh oon beek-KYEH-reh ah-lah JOY-ah eh ah-lah feh-lee-CHEE-tah keh por-TYA-mo NEL-le NO-streh VEE-teh ree-kroh-PRO-khe.]

8. "Here's to our love story, filled with beautiful chapters yet to be written." - "Brindiamo alla nostra storia d'amore, ricca di splendidi capitoli ancora da scrivere." [breen-DEE-ah-moh ahl-la NO-streh STO-ree-ah dah-MOH-reh, REEK-kah dee splehn-DEE-dee ka-PEE-toh-lee ahn-KOH-rah dah skree-VEH-reh.]

9. "Cheers to the wonderful moments we've shared and the ones yet to come." - "Salute ai meravigliosi momenti che abbiamo condiviso e a quelli che verranno." [sa-LOO-teh ah-ee meh-rah-VEE-glee-oh-zee moh-MEN-tee keh ahb-BYA-moh kon-DEE-vee-zoh eh ah KWEHL-lee keh veh-RAN-no.]

10. "Let's toast to our love, which grows stronger with each passing day." - "Brindiamo al nostro amore, che si rafforza sempre di più ogni giorno che passa." [breen-DEE-ah-moh al NO-stro a-MOH-reh, keh see raf-FOR-tsa SEM-preh dee pyoo OH-nyee JOR-no keh PAS-sa.]

PHRASES FOR DISCUSSING FUTURE PLANS TOGETHER

1. "Where do you see us in five years?" - "Dove ci vedi tra cinque anni?" [DOH-veh chee VEH-dee trah CHEEN-kweh AHN-nee?]

2. "I hope we can travel the world together someday." - "Spero che un giorno possiamo viaggiare insieme per il mondo." [SPEH-roh keh oon JOR-no pohs-SYA-mo vyah-JAH-reh een-SYE-meh pehr eel MOHN-doh.]

3. "Let's make plans for our dream house." - "Facciamo dei piani per la nostra casa dei sogni." [FAH-chya-mo deey PYAH-nee pehr la NO-streh KAH-zah dey SOH-nyee.]

4. "What adventures do you want to experience together?" - "Quali avventure vorresti vivere insieme?" [KWAH-lee ahv-ven-TOO-reh voh-RES-tee vee-VEH-reh een-SYE-meh?]

5. "Let's set goals and work towards them as a team." - "Fissiamo degli obiettivi e lavoriamo insieme per raggiungerli." [FEESS-see-ah-mo DEY-ee oh-BYEH-tee-vee eh la-vo-REE-ah-mo een-SYE-meh pehr rah-JOON-ghehr-lee.]

6. "I see us building a life filled with love and happiness." - "Mi immagino noi che costruiamo una vita piena d'amore e felicità." [Mee eem-MAH-gee-no noy keh koh-STROO-yah-mo OO-nah VEE-tah PYEH-nah dah-MOH-reh eh feh-lee-CHEE-tah.]

7. "Let's talk about our career aspirations and how we can support each other." - "Parliamo delle nostre aspirazioni professionali e di come possiamo sostenerci a vicenda." [PAR-lee-ah-mo DEY-lee NO-streh ah-spee-rah-ZYO-nee pro-fes-syoh-NAH-lee eh dee KOH-meh pohs-SYA-mo so-steh-NEHR-chee ah vee-CHEHN-dah.]

8. "What kind of family do you envision for us?" - "Che tipo di famiglia immagini per noi?" [Keh TEE-po dee fah-MEEL-yah ee-MMAH-jee-nee pehr noy?]

9. "Let's make plans for our next vacation together." - "Facciamo dei piani per la nostra prossima vacanza insieme." [FAH-chya-mo deey PYAH-nee pehr la NO-strah PROHS-see-mah vah-KAHN-tsah een-SYE-meh.]
10. "I can't wait to see what the future holds for us." - "Non vedo l'ora di vedere cosa ci riserva il futuro." [Non VEH-doh LOH-rah dee veh-DEH-reh KOH-zah chee ree-SER-vah eel foo-TOO-roh.

19

SPORTING EVENTS

It makes no difference if you're going to Italy to watch a football game, a tennis tournament, or any other type of sporting event; knowing a few essential phrases can make your time there more pleasurable and will help you interact with other people who share your passion for sports.

In this chapter, we will examine a range of phrases that will enable you to cheer for your team, support the athletes, and engage in talks about the game.

WORDS REFERRING TO SPORTS

1. "Football" - "Calcio" - [KAHL-tchoh]
2. "Basketball" - "Pallacanestro" - [pal-la-ka-NES-troh]
3. "Tennis" - "Tennis" - [TEN-nis]
4. "Swimming" - "Nuoto" - [NOO-oh-toh]
5. "Running" - "Corsa" - [KOR-sah]
6. "Cycling" - "Ciclismo" - [chee-KLIS-moh]
7. "Golf" - "Golf" - [golf]

8. "Soccer" - "Calcio" - [KAHL-tchoh]
9. "Volleyball" - "Pallavolo" - [pal-la-VO-loh]
10. "Baseball" - "Baseball" - [BEYS-bawl]
11. "Hockey" - "Hockey" - [HAWK-ee]
12. "Gymnastics" - "Ginnastica" - [gee-nahs-TEE-kah]
13. "Boxing" - "Pugilato" - [poo-jee-LAH-toh]
14. "Wrestling" - "Lotta" - [LOT-tah]
15. "Martial arts" - "Arti marziali" - [AR-tee mar-TSYAH-lee]
16. "Athletics" - "Atletica" - [at-leh-TEE-kah]
17. "Horse riding" - "Equitazione" - [eh-kwee-tsee-TSAH-zeeoh-neh]
18. "Skiing" - "Sci" - [skee]
19. "Surfing" - "Surf" - [serf]
20. "Yoga" - "Yoga" - [YOH-gah]

VOCABULARY FOR VARIOUS SPORTS

1. "Football (soccer) is a popular sport in Italy." - "Il Calcio è uno sport popolare in Italia." [Eel KAHL-choh eh OOH-noh sport po-poh-LAH-reh een ee-TAH-lyah.]
2. "Tennis is played on a tennis court." - "Il tennis si gioca su un campo da tennis." [Eel TEN-nees see JOH-kah soo oon KAHM-poh dah TEN-nees.]
3. "Basketball is a fast-paced sport." - "La pallacanestro è uno sport veloce." [lah pahl-lah-ka-NEH-stroh eh OOH-noh sport veh-LOH-cheh.]
4. "Cycling is a popular sport in the mountains." - "Il ciclismo è uno sport popolare in montagna." [Eel chee-CLEEZ-moh eh OOH-noh sport po-poh-LAH-reh een mohn-TAHN-yah.]
5. "Swimming is great for staying fit." - "Nuotare fa bene per mantenersi in forma." [Nwoh-TAH-reh fah BEH-neh pehr mahn-teh-NEHR-see een FOHR-mah.]
6. "Golf is played on a golf course." - "Il golf si gioca su un campo da golf." - [Eel golf see JOH-kah soo oon KAHM-poh dah golf.]
7. "Athletics includes running, jumping, and throwing." - "L'atletica comprende corsa, salto e lancio." [Laht-leh-TEE-kah kohm-PREHN-deh KOHR-sah, SAHL-toh eh LAHN-choh.]
8. "Volleyball is played on a volleyball court." - "La pallavolo si gioca su un campo da pallavolo." [Lah pahl-lah-VOH-loh see JOH-kah soo oon KAHM-poh dah pahl-lah-VOH-loh.]
9. "Rugby is a physical contact sport." - "Il rugby è uno sport di contatto fisico." [Eel ROO-bee eh OOH-noh sport dee kohn-TAHT-toh FEE-zee-koh.]
10. "Motorsports, like Formula 1, are thrilling to watch." - "Gli sport motoristici, come la Formula 1, sono emozionanti da vedere." [Glee sport moh-toh-rees-TEE-chee, KOH-meh lah FooR-moo-lah OO-noh, SOH-noh eh-moh-tsyoh-NAHN-tee dah veh-DEH-reh.]

1. "Italy has a strong soccer tradition." - "L'Italia ha una forte tradizione calcistica." [Lee-TAH-lyah ah OO-nah FOHR-teh trah-dee-ZEEOH-neh kahl-KEES-tee-kah.]
2. "What team do you root for?" - "Per che squadra tifi?" [Per kee skwah-dra TEE-fee?]
3. "The match was intense and exciting." - "La partita è stata intensa ed emozionante." [La pahr-TEE-tah eh STAH-tah een-TEHN-sah ehd eh-moh-tsyoh-NAHN-teh.]
4. "Did you see that amazing goal?" - "Hai visto quel gol fantastico?" [Ee VEE-stoh kwehl gohl fahn-TAH-stee-koh?]
5. "The goalkeeper made a fantastic save." - "Il portiere ha fatto un salvataggio fantastico." [Eel pohr-TYEH-reh ah FAHT-toh oon sahl-vah-TAH-joh fahn-TAH-stee-koh.]
6. "The referee made a controversial decision." - "L'arbitro ha preso una decisione controversa." [Lahr-BEE-troh ah PREH-zoh OO-nah dee-zee-ZEEOH-neh kohn-troh-VEHR-sah.]
7. "The crowd was cheering loudly throughout the match." - "La folla ha applaudito rumorosamente per tutta la partita." [La FOHL-lah ah ah-plow-DEE-toh roo-moh-roh-SAH-mehn-teh pehr TOOT-tah lah pahr-TEE-tah.]
8. "It was a thrilling game with many exciting moments." - "È stata una partita emozionante con molti momenti entusiasmanti." [Eh STAH-tah OO-nah pahr-TEE-tah eh-moh-tsyoh-NAHN-teh kohn MOHL-tee moh-MEHN-tee ehn-too-zee-AH-sman-tee.]
9. "The team played with great teamwork and coordination." - "La squadra ha giocato con grande lavoro di squadra e coordinazione." [La SKWAH-drah ah joh-KAH-toh kohn GRAHN-deh la-VOH-roh dee SKWAH-drah eh KOHR-dee-nah-TSYOH-neh.]
10. "Soccer unites people from all walks of life." - "Il calcio unisce le persone di ogni estrazione sociale." [Eel kahl-CHOH oo-NEE-sheh leh pehr-SOH-neh dee OH-nyee eh-stra-TSYOH-neh soh-KAH-leh.]

ASKING FOR TICKETS OR INFORMATION ABOUT A SPORTING EVENT

1. "Excuse me, where can I buy tickets for the game?" - "Mi scusi, dove posso comprare i biglietti per la partita?" [Mee SKOO-zee, DOH-veh POHs-soh kohm-PRAH-reh ee beel-YET-tee pehr lah pahr-TEE-tah?]
2. "How much do the tickets cost?" - "Quanto costano i biglietti?" [KWAHN-toh koh-STAH-noh ee beel-YET-tee?]
3. "Is there a discount for children or seniors?" - "Ci sono sconti per bambini o anziani?" [Chee SOH-noh SKOHN-tee pehr bahm-BEE-nee oh ahn-TSYAH-nee?]

4. "Can I reserve tickets in advance?" - "Posso prenotare i biglietti in anticipo?" [POHs-soh preh-noh-TAH-reh ee beel-YET-tee een ahn-TEE-chee-poh?]
5. "Are there any VIP or premium seating options available?" - "Ci sono opzioni di posti VIP o premium disponibili?" [Chee SOH-noh ohp-TSYOH-nee dee POH-stee VIP oh PREH-mee-oom dees-poh-NEE-bee-lee?]
6. "When does the game start?" - "Quando inizia la partita?"[KWAHN-doh een-EE-tsah lah pahr-TEE-tah?]
7. "Is there parking available near the stadium?" - "Ci sono parcheggi disponibili vicino allo stadio?" [Chee SOH-noh pahr-KEH-jee dees-poh-NEE-bee-lee vee-CHEE-noh AHL-loh STAH-dyoh?]
8. "Can I bring my own food and drinks to the stadium?" - "Posso portare il mio cibo e le bevande allo stadio?" [POHs-soh pohr-TAH-reh eel MEE-oh KOH-boh eh leh beh-VAHN-deh AHL-loh STAH-dyoh?]
9. "Are there any restrictions on bringing bags or backpacks into the stadium?" - "Ci sono restrizioni per l'ingresso di borse o zaini allo stadio?" [Chee SOH-noh reh-STREE-tsyoh-nee pehr leen-GREHS-soh dee BOHR-seh oh ZAH-ee-nee AHL-loh STAH-dyoh?]
10. "Where can I find more information about the upcoming matches?" - "Dove posso trovare ulteriori informazioni sulle prossime partite?" [DOH-veh POHs-soh troh-VAH-reh ool-tee-RYOH-ree een-fohr-mah-TSYOH-nee SOHL-leh PROS-see-meh pahr-TEE-teh?]

EXPRESSING ENTHUSIASM DURING A GAME

1. "Wow, what a great goal!" - "Wow, che gol fantastico!" [Wow, keh gol fahn-TAH-stee-koh!]
2. "That was an incredible save by the goalkeeper!" - "Quella è stata una parata incredibile del portiere!" [KWEH-lah eh STAH-tah OO-nah pah-RAH-tah een-KREH-dee-bee-leh del pohr-TYEH-reh!]
3. "We're winning! Keep up the good work!" - "Stiamo vincendo! Continuate così!" [STYAH-moh veen-CHEHN-doh! Kohn-tee-noo-AH-teh KOH-zee!]
4. "The atmosphere in the stadium is electric!" - "L'atmosfera nello stadio è elettrica!" [LAH-tohsmeh-rah NEHL-loh STAH-dyoh eh eh-LEH-tree-kah!]
5. "I can't believe how talented these players are!" - "Non posso credere quanto sono talentuosi questi giocatori!" [Non POHs-so kreh-DEH-reh KWAHN-toh SOH-noh tah-lehn-TOO-oh-zee KWEH-stee joh-KAH-toh-ree!]
6. "This is such an intense match!" - "Questa partita è così intensa!" [KWEH-stah pahr-TEE-tah eh KOH-zee een-TEHN-sah!]
7. "The crowd is going wild!" - "La folla è fuori di testa!" [La FOL-lah eh FWOH-ree dee TEH-stah!]

8. "What a fantastic play by our team!" - "Che giocata fantastica della nostra squadra!" [Keh joh-KAH-tah fahn-TAH-stee-kah DEHL-lah NOS-trah SKWAH-drah!]

9. "I'm on the edge of my seat!" - "Sono sulle spine!" [SOH-noh SOOL-leh SPEE-neh!]

10. "This is the best game I've ever seen!" - "Questa è la migliore partita che abbia mai visto!" [KWEH-stah eh lah meel-YOH-reh pahr-TEE-tah keh AHB-bee-ah mah-ee VEE-stoh!]

POST-GAME DIALOGUES AT THE BAR

1. "What a thrilling game!" - "Che partita emozionante!" [Che pa-REE-ta e-mo-tsee-o-NAN-te!]

2. "We played really well tonight." - "Abbiamo giocato davvero bene stasera." [Ab-BEE-a-mo jo-KA-to moo-YE bEY-ney stA-se-RA.]

3. "Did you see that amazing goal?" - "Hai visto quel gol fantastico?" [Ha-ee vee-STO kwehl gol faN-TAS-ti-co?]

4. "It was a tough match, but we gave it our all." - È stata una partita difficile, ma abbiamo dato il massimo. [Eh sta-ta o-na par-TEE-ta DIF-fi-chi-ley, ma ab-BEE-a-mo DA-to eel MAs-si-mo.]

5. "Let's celebrate our victory!" - "Festeggiamo la nostra vittoria! "- [Fes-te-GGEE-a-mo la no-STRA veet-TO-rya!]

6. "The atmosphere at the stadium was incredible." - "L'atmosfera allo stadio era incredibile." [L'at-mo-SE-fe-ra al-LO sta-DEE-o e-rah een-KRE-di-bi-ley.]

7. "I can't believe we won in the last minute!" - "Non posso credere che abbiamo vinto all'ultimo minuto!" [Non po-so cre-DEY-ey che ab-BEE-a-mo vee-NEY-to neyL UL-tee-mo mi-NOO-to!]

8. "Our team showed great teamwork and skill." - "La nostra squadra ha dimostrato un grande spirito di squadra e abilità."[La no-STRA squa-DRA o mo-stra-to GRAN-dey LAVO-ro dEE-si-plee-na e A-bee-LEE-ta.]

9. "We have such passionate fans." - "Abbiamo dei tifosi così appassionati." [Ab-BEE-a-mo DEE tif-O-zee co-SE app-a-syo-NA-tee.]

10. "What an exciting game to remember!" - "Che partita emozionante da ricordare!" [Che pa-REE-ta e-mo-tsee-o-NAN-te da ri-koR-DA-rey!]

IN CASE OF EMERGENCY

In this chapter, we will explore essential phrases and vocabulary to help you communicate effectively in emergency situations. Whether you find yourself in need of medical assistance, reporting a crime, or seeking help during a natural disaster, knowing the right words can make a crucial difference. This comprehensive guide will equip you with the necessary language skills to navigate emergency scenarios and ensure your safety and well-being.

COMMONLY USED WORDS IN EMERGENCY SITUATIONS

1. "Emergency" - "Emergenza" - [eh-MER-jen-tsah]
2. "Help" - "Aiuto" - [ai-OO-toh]
3. "Ambulance" - "Ambulanza" - [ahm-boo-LAHN-tsah]
4. "Fire" - "Fuoco" - [FWOH-koh]
5. "Police" - "Polizia" - [poh-LEE-tsyah]
6. "Injury" - "Lesione" - [leh-SYO-neh]
7. "Accident" - "Incidente" - [een-CHEE-den-teh]

8. "Pain" - "Dolore" - [DO-loh-reh]
9. "Bleeding" - "Sanguinamento" - [san-gwee-nah-MEN-toh]
10. "Broken" - "Rotto" - [RO-toh]
11. "Danger" - "Pericolo" - [peh-REE-koh-loh]
12. "Evacuate" - "Evacuare" - [eh-vah-koo-AH-reh]
13. "Rescue" - "Salvataggio" - [sal-va-TA-djoh]
14. "Hospital" - "Ospedale" - [os-pe-DA-leh]
15. "First aid" - "Primo soccorso" - [PREE-moh sok-KOR-soh]
16. "Disaster" - "Disastro" - [dee-ZAS-troh]
17. "Safety" - "Sicurezza" - [see-koo-RET-tsah]
18. "Shelter" - "Rifugio" - [ree-FOO-djoh]

ASKING FOR HELP IN VARIOUS SITUATIONS

1. "Excuse me, can you help me? I'm lost." - "Mi scusi, può aiutarmi? Mi sono perso/a." [mee SKOO-see, pwoh eye-oo-TAR-mee? Mee so-no pehr-soh/a]
2. "Please, call an ambulance. There's been an accident." - "Per favore, chiami un'ambulanza. C'è stato un incidente." [pair fa-VOH-re, KYAH-mee oon am-boo-LAN-tsa. Cheh STAH-toh oon in-chee-DEN-te]
3. "I need help. My wallet has been stolen." - "Ho bisogno di aiuto. Mi hanno rubato il portafoglio." [oh bee-ZO-nyoh dee eye-oo-TOH. Mee AH-noh roo-BAH-toh eel por-ta-FOHL-yoh]
4. "Is there a police station nearby? I need to report a crime." - "C'è una stazione di polizia nelle vicinanze? Devo denunciare un crimine." [cheh OOH-nah sta-TSYOH-neh dee po-LEE-tzyah nel-leh vee-chee-NAN-tse? DEH-vo deh-noon-CHA-re oon kree-MEE-neh]
5. "Can you please help me find a pharmacy? I'm not feeling well." - "Può aiutarmi a trovare una farmacia? Non mi sento bene." [pwoh eye-oo-TAR-mee a tro-VA-reh OOH-nah far-MA-kyah? Non mee SEN-toh BEH-neh]
6. "Excuse me, is there a fire extinguisher nearby? There's a small fire." - "Scusi, c'è un estintore nelle vicinanze? C'è un piccolo incendio." [SKOO-see, cheh oon es-tin-TOH-reh nel-leh vee-chee-NAN-tse? Cheh oon pee-COH-lo in-CEN-dio]
7. "Help! There's been an accident. Call the police." - "Aiuto! C'è stato un incidente. Chiami la polizia." [eye-OO-toh! Cheh STAH-toh oon in-CHEE-den-te. KYAH-mee la po-LEE-tzyah]
8. "Please, I need a doctor. I'm feeling very sick." - "Per favore, ho bisogno di un medico. Mi sento molto male." [pair fa-VOH-re, oh bee-ZO-nyoh dee oon MEH-dee-coh. Mee SEN-toh MOHL-toh MAH-leh]
9. "Is there a hospital nearby? I need urgent medical assistance." - "C'è un ospedale nelle vicinanze? Ho bisogno di assistenza medica urgente." [cheh OON os-peh-DA-leh nel-leh vee-chee-NAN-tse? Oh bee-ZO-nyoh dee assis-TEN-za MEH-di-ca oor-GEN-te]

10. "Excuse me, can you help me find the nearest embassy? I've lost my passport." - "Mi scusi, può aiutarmi a trovare l'ambasciata più vicina? Ho perso il mio passaporto." [mee SKOO-see, pwò eye-oo-TAR-mee a tro-VA-re lam-ba-SHA-ta PYOO vee-CHI-na? OH PEHR-so eel MEE-o pas-sa-POR-to]

PHRASES TO DESCRIBE MEDICAL SYMPTOMS

1. "I have a fever and chills." - "Ho la febbre e brividi." [oh lah FEB-breh eh bree-VEE-dee]
2. "I'm experiencing chest pain and difficulty breathing." - "Ho dolore al petto e difficoltà respiratorie." [oh doh-LOH-reh al PEH-toh eh dee-fee-kohl-TAH ree-spi-ra-TOH- ree-eh]
3. "I feel dizzy and lightheaded." - "Mi sento stordito/a e confuso/a." [mee SEN-toh stor-DEE-toh/ah eh kon-FOO-soh/ah]
4. "I have a persistent cough and sore throat." - "Ho una tosse persistente e mal di gola." [oh oo-na TOHS-seh per-sis-TEN-teh eh mal dee GOH-lah]
5. "I'm experiencing nausea and vomiting." - "Ho nausea e vomito." [oh NAU-zya eh VOH-mee-toh]
6. "I have a rash and itching on my skin." - "Ho una eruzione cutanea e prurito sulla pelle." [oh OO-na eh-roo-TSYOH-neh koo-tah-NEH-ah eh proo-REE-toh SOO-lah PEHL-leh]
7. "I feel weak and fatigued." - "Mi sento debole e affaticato/a." [mee SEN-toh DEH-boh-leh eh af-fa-tee-KAH-toh/ah]
8. "I have a severe headache and sensitivity to light." - "Ho un forte mal di testa e sensibilità alla luce." [oh oon FOR-teh mal dee TEH-stah eh sen-see-bee-lee-TAH ALL-lah LOO-tche]
9. "I'm experiencing stomach pain and diarrhea." - "Ho mal di stomaco e diarrea." [oh mal dee sto-MAH-koh eh DYAH-reh-ah]
10. "I have swelling and pain in my joints." - "Ho gonfiore e dolore alle articolazioni." [oh gon-FYO-reh eh doh-LOH-reh ALL-leh ar-tee-coh-LAH-tsyoh-nee]

DIALOGUE WITH THE POLICE

1. "Excuse me, officer. I need your help." - "Mi scusi, agente. Ho bisogno del suo aiuto." [mee SKOO-zee, ah-JEN-teh. oh bee-ZOH-nyoh del soo-oh ah-YOO-toh]
2. "I've been a victim of theft. Can you assist me?" - "Sono stato/a vittima di furto. Può aiutarmi?" [SOH-noh STAH-toh/ah VEET-tee-mah dee FOOR-toh. pwoh ah-YOO-tar-mee]
3. "I witnessed an accident. What should I do?" - "Ho assistito a un incidente. Cosa dovrei fare?" [oh ah-see-STEE-toh ah oon een-chee-DEN-teh. KOH-zah doh-VREH-ee FAH-reh]

4. "I've lost my passport. How can I report it?" - "Ho perso il mio passaporto. Come posso denunciarlo?" [oh PEHR-so eel MEE-oh pass-ah-POR-toh. KOH-meh POS-soh deh-noon-CHYAH-rloh]
5. "There's been a break-in at my apartment. Please come quickly." - "C'è stato un intrusione nel mio appartamento. Venga presto, per favore." [CHEH STAH-toh oon een-troo-ZYOH-neh nel MEE-oh ap-par-tah-MEN-toh. VEN-gah PREHS-toh, per FAH-voh-reh]
6. "I need to file a police report for the incident." - "Ho bisogno di fare una denuncia per l'incidente." [oh bee-ZOH-nyoh dee FAH-reh oo-nah deh-noon-CHYAH per leen-chee-DEN-teh]
7. "Can you provide me with your badge number and contact information?" - "Può fornirmi il suo numero di targa e le informazioni di contatto?" [pwoh for-NEER-mee eel SOO-oh NOO-meh-roh dee TAR-gah eh leh een-for-mah-TSYOH-nee dee kon-TAHK-toh]
8. "I'm a witness to a crime. Can you take my statement?" - "Sono un testimone di un reato. Può prendere la mia dichiarazione?" [SOH-noh oon teh-SEE-moh-neh dee oon re-AH-toh. pwoh prehn-DEH-reh lah MEE-ah dee-kee-lah-rah-TSYOH-neh]
9. "I need help finding a lost child. Can you assist me in the search?" - "Ho bisogno di aiuto per trovare un bambino smarrito. Può aiutarmi nelle ricerche?" [oh bee-ZOH-nyoh dee ah-YOO-toh per troh-VAH-reh oon bam-BEE-noh smar-REE-toh. pwoh ah-YOO-tar-mee NEHL-leh ree-CHEHR-keh]
10. "Thank you for your prompt response and assistance." - "Grazie per la pronta risposta e l'aiuto." [GRAHT-zyeh per lah PRON-tah ree-SPOHS-tah eh lai-OO-toh]

CONTACT THE EMBASSY OR CONSULATE

1. "I need to contact my embassy. Can you provide me with their contact information?" - "Ho bisogno di contattare la mia ambasciata. Può fornirmi le informazioni di contatto?" [oh bee-ZOH-nyo dee kon-tat-TAH-reh lah MEE-ah am-ba-SHAH-tah. pwoh for-NEER-mee leh een-for-ma-TSYOH-nee dee kon-TAHK-toh]
2. "I've lost my passport. What should I do? Can the embassy help me?" - "Ho perso il mio passaporto. Cosa dovrei fare? Può l'ambasciata aiutarmi?" [oh PEHR-soh eel MEE-oh pas-sa-POR-toh. KOH-zah doh-VREH-ee FAH-reh? pwoh lam-ba-SHAH-tah ah-YOO-tar-mee]
3. "I've been involved in an emergency situation. I need assistance from my consulate." - "Sono stato/a coinvolto/a in una situazione di emergenza. Ho bisogno di assistenza dal mio consolato." [SOH-noh STAH-toh/ah koh-ee-NVOHL-toh/ah een OO-nah see-too-ah-TSYOH-neh dee e-mer-JEN-tzah. oh bee-ZOH-nyoh dee ah-yoo-STEN-tzah dahl MEE-oh kon-soh-LAH-toh]
4. "Can you provide me with the address and phone number of my embassy/consulate?" - "Può fornirmi l'indirizzo e il numero di telefono

della mia ambasciata/consolato?" [pwoh for-NEER-mee leen-dee-REE-tso e eel NOO-meh-roh dee te-leh-FOH-noh DEL-lah MEE-ah am-ba-SHAH-tah/kon-soh-LAH-toh]

5. "I've had my belongings stolen. Can the consulate assist me in reporting the incident?" - "Mi hanno rubato i miei effetti personali. Può il consolato aiutarmi a denunciare l'incidente?" [mee AHN-noh roo-BAH-toh ee MEE-eh ef-FEH-tee per-soh-NAH-lee. pwoh eel kon-soh-LAH-toh ah-yoo-TAR-mee ah deh-noon-CHA-reh leen-chee- DEHN-teh]

6. "I've lost my wallet and identification documents. Can the consulate help me with replacement documents?" - "Ho perso il portafoglio e i documenti di identificazione. Il consolato può aiutarmi a ottenere documenti sostitutivi?" [oh PEHR-soh eel por-tah-FOH-lyoh ee ee do-koo-MEN-tee dee een-tee-fee-ka-TSYOH-neh. eel kon-soh-LAH-toh pwoh ah-YOO-tar-mee ah oh-teh-NEH-reh do-koo-MEN-tee soh-see-too-TEE-vee]

7. "I've been a victim of a crime. Can the embassy guide me on what steps to take?" - "Sono stato/a vittima di un crimine. L'ambasciata può guidarmi su quali passi seguire?" [SOH-noh STAH-toh/ah VEET-tee-mah dee oon kree-MEE-neh. lam-ba-SHAH-tah pwoh GWEE-dar-mee soo KWAH-lee PAH-see se-GWEE-reh]

8. "I've had a medical emergency. Can the consulate assist me in finding medical help?" - "Ho avuto un'emergenza medica. Il consolato può aiutarmi a trovare assistenza medica?" [oh ah-VOO-toh oon eh-mer-JEN-zah MEH-dee-kah. eel kon-soh-LAH-toh pwoh ah-YOO-tar-mee ah tro-VAH-reh ah-sis-TEN-tzah MEH- dee-kah]

9. "I've lost my travel documents. Can the embassy provide me with temporary travel documents?" - "Ho perso i documenti di viaggio. L'ambasciata può fornirmi documenti di viaggio temporanei?" [oh PEHR-soh ee do-koo-MEN-tee dee vee-AH-joh. lam-ba-SHAH-tah pwoh for-NEER-mee do-koo-MEN-tee dee vee-AH-joh tem-po-rah-NEH-ee]

10. "I've encountered a legal issue. Can the consulate offer legal advice or connect me with a lawyer?" - "Ho avuto un problema legale. Il consolato può offrire consulenza legale o mettermi in contatto con un avvocato?" [oh ah-VOO-toh oon pro-BLEH-mah leh-GAH-le. eel kon-soh-LAH-toh pwoh off-REE-reh kon-soo-LEN-tzah leh-GAH-le o meh-TER-mee een kon-TAHK-toh kon oon ah-vvoh- KAH-toh]

You should immediately contact your country's embassy or consulate for specific assistance in case of emergencies or problems while traveling. Contact information for the embassy or consulate can be found on your country's official website or through the Ministry of Foreign Affairs.

1. "My car has broken down. Can you send a tow truck?" - "La mia macchina si è guastata. Puoi mandare un carro attrezzi?" [la MEE-a ma-KEE-na see eh gwah-STA-ta. pwoy man-DA-re oon KAR-ro at-TRETS-see]
2. "I have a flat tire. Is there a service station nearby?" - "Ho una gomma a terra. C'è una stazione di servizio nelle vicinanze?" [oh OO-na GOM-ma a TEH-ra. chey OO-na sta-TSYO-neh dee ser-VEE-tsyoh NEHL-leh vee-chi-NAN-tse]
3. "I've run out of gas. Is there a gas station close by?" - "Mi sono rimasto senza benzina. C'è un distributore di benzina qui vicino?" [mee SO-noh ree-MAHS-to SEN-za ben-ZEE-na. chey oon dees-tree-BOO-to-re dee ben-ZEE-na KWI vee-CHEE-no]
4. "I've locked my keys in the car. Can you help me with a locksmith?" - "Ho lasciato le chiavi dentro la macchina. Puoi aiutarmi con un fabbro?" [oh lah-SHYAH-toh leh KYAH-vee DEN-troh la ma-KEE-na. pwoy ah-YOO-tar-mee kon oon FAB-bro]
5. "My car battery is dead. Do you have jumper cables?" - "La mia batteria dell'auto è scarica. Hai dei cavi per far partire l'auto?" [la MEE-a ba-TAY-ree-a del-LAU-to eh ska-REE-ka. a-ee DAY ka-VEE per far par-TEE-reh LAU-to]
6. "I've had a minor accident. Can you call the police for me?" - "Ho avuto un incidente minore. Puoi chiamare la polizia per me?" [oh a-VOO-toh oon in-CHEE-dente mee-NO-re. pwoy kya-MA-reh la po-LEE-tsyah per me]
7. "I've lost my wallet. Is there a police station nearby to report it?" - "Ho perso il portafoglio. C'è una stazione di polizia qui vicino per fare una denuncia?" [oh PER-so eel por-ta-FOH-lyo. chey OO-na sta-TSYO-neh dee po-LEE-tsyah KWI vee-CHEE-no per FA-reh OO-na den-TSYOO-neh]
8. "I've been pickpocketed. Can you assist me in contacting my embassy?" - "Sono stato derubato. Puoi aiutarmi a contattare la mia ambasciata?" [SO-no STA-to de-ROO-ba-to. pwoy ah-YOO-tar-mee a kon-TAH-ta-reh la MEE-a am-ba-SYAH-ta]
9. "I need to file a police report. Where can I do that?" - "Ho bisogno di fare una denuncia alla polizia. Dove posso farlo?" [oh bee-ZO-nyo dee FAH-reh OO-na den-TSYOO-neh AH-lah po-LEE-tsyah. DO-veh POH-so FAR-lo]
10. "I've witnessed a crime. Is there an officer I can speak to?" - "Ho assistito a un crimine. C'è un agente con cui posso parlare?" [oh ah-SIS-tee-to a oon KREE-meh. chey oon ah-JEN-teh kon KWI POH-so par-LAH-reh]

In case of emergencies, immediately contact the local emergency number (118 for a medical emergency, 113 for police, 115 for firefighters) and follow the instructions of the relevant authorities.

TRAVELLING BY AIR

This chapter will provide you with a set of useful phrases to help you best deal with your airport experience.

It is critical to feel safe and comfortable while traveling, whether you are leaving for a new experience or coming home.

You will learn how to request information, check in, go through security, get assistance, and understand relevant directions.

With the help of this chapter, you will be able to communicate effectively with airport staff and move through the complex airport environment with ease.

Get ready for a smooth travel experience and enjoy your flight!

COMMON WORDS OF AIR TRAVEL

1. "Aircraft" - "Aeromobile" - [eh-roh-mo-BEE-leh]
2. "Flight" - "Volo" - [VOH-loh]
3. "Passenger" - "Passeggero" - [pahs-seh-DJEH-roh]
4. "Airport" - "Aeroporto" - [ah-eh-roh-POR-toh]

5. "Boarding" - "Imbarco" - [im-BAR-ko]
6. "Takeoff" - "Decollo" - [deh-KOL-loh]
7. "Landing" - "Atterraggio" - [at-teh-RAJ-jo]
8. "Security" - "Sicurezza" - [see-koo-RET-tsah]
9. "Baggage" - "Bagaglio" - [bah-GA-lyoh]
10. "Seat" - "Posto" - [PO-stoh]
11. "Cabin" - "Cabina" - [KA-bee-nah]
12. "Pilot" - "Pilota" - [pee-LOH-tah]
13. "Crew" - "Equipaggio" - [eh-kwee-PAJ-jo]
14. "Passport" - "Passaporto" - [pahs-sa-POR-toh]
15. "Visa" - "Visto" - [VEE-stoh]
16. "Departure" - "Partenza" - [par-TEN-tsah]
17. "Arrival" - "Arrivo" - [ah-REE-voh]
18. "Delay" - "Ritardo" - [ree-TAR-doh]
19. "Gate" - "Varco" - [VAR-koh]
20. "In-flight" - "Durante il volo" - [doo-RAN-te eel VOH-lo]
21. "Airline" - "Compagnia aerea" - [kom-PAH-nyah ah-EH-reh-ah]
22. "Ticket" - "Biglietto" - [beel-LYET-toh]
23. "Cabin crew" - "Equipaggio di cabina" - [eh-kwee-PAJ-jo dee KA-bee-nah]
24. "In-flight entertainment" - "Intrattenimento a bordo" - [een-fleet en-ter-TEYN-mehnt oh BOR-doh]
25. "Turbulence" - "Turbolenza" - [ter-boh-LEN-tsah]
26. "Overhead compartment" - "Scomparto sopra la testa" - [skom-PAR-toh SO-prah lah TEHS-tah]
27. "Emergency exit" - "Uscita di emergenza" - [oo-SHEE-tah dee eh-mehr-DJEN-tsah]
28. "Cockpit" - "Cabina di pilotaggio" - [kah-BEE-nah dee pee-loh-TA-joh]
29. "Air traffic control" - "Controllo del traffico aereo" - [kon-TROL-lo del TRAF-fee-koh ah-EH-reh-oh]
30. "In-flight meal" - "Pasto a bordo" - [PA-stoh ah BOR-doh]
31. "Immigration" - "Immigrazione" - [im-mee-gra-TSYOH-neh]
32. "Customs" - "Dogana" - [doh-GAH-nah]
33. "Baggage claim" - "Ritiro bagagli" - [ree-TEE-roh bah-GA-lyee]
34. "Lost luggage" - "Bagaglio smarrito" - [bah-GA-lyoh s-ma-REET-toh]
35. "Flight attendant" - "Assistente di volo" - [ah-see-STEN-te dee VOH-loh]
36. "Runway" - "Pista" - [PEES-tah]
37. "Jet lag" - "Sindrome da fuso orario" - [sin-DRO-meh dah FOO-zoh o-RAH-ree-oh]
38. "Connecting flight" - "Volo di collegamento" - [VOH-loh dee kol-leh-ga-MEN-toh]
39. "Window seat" - "Posto vicino al finestrino" - [PO-stoh vee-CHEE-no ahl fee-neh-STREE-noh]
40. "Cabin pressure" - "Pressione cabina" - [pre-SEE-oh-neh kah-BEE-nah]

VOCABULARY FOR CHECK-IN AND BOARDING

1. "I would like to check-in for my flight, please." - "Vorrei effettuare il check-in per il mio volo, per favore." [Vor-REY ef-fet-TWA-rey il chek-in per il MEE-o VO-lo, per fa-VO-re.]
2. "Where can I find the check-in counter?" - "Dove posso trovare il banco del check-in?" [DO-vey POS-so tro-VAR-rey il BAN-ko del chek-in?]
3. "I have a reservation under the name Smith." - "Ho una prenotazione a nome Smith." [O oo-NA pre-no-ta-TSYO-ney a NO-mey Smith.]
4. "What is the weight limit for checked baggage?" - "Qual è il limite di peso per il bagaglio da stiva?" [Kwal ey il LI-mi-tey dee PE-so per il ba-GAL-lyo da STI-va?]
5. "Can I have a window seat, please?" - "Posso avere un posto vicino al finestrino, per favore?" [POS-so a-VE-rey oon PO-sto vee-CHEE-no al fee-NES-tree-no, per fa-VO-re.]
6. "Is there an extra fee for oversized baggage?" - "C'è un costo aggiuntivo per i bagagli fuori misura?" [Cheh oon CO-sto ad-JOON-tee-vo per ee ba-GA-lyee FWO-ree MEE-ZU-ra?]
7. "I need to declare items in my baggage." - "Devo dichiarare degli oggetti nel mio bagaglio." [DE-vo dee-kyar-A-rey DEY-ee OBYET-tee nel MEE-o ba-GA-lyo.]
8. "Can I have a boarding pass, please?" - "Posso avere una carta d'imbarco, per favore?" [POS-so a-VE-rey OO-na CAR-ta deem-BAR-ko, per fa-VO-re.]
9. "What is the gate number for my flight?" - "Qual è il numero del gate per il mio volo?" [Kwal ey il NOO-me-ro del GEYT per il MEE-o VO-lo?]
10. "Is there any priority boarding for families with children?" - "C'è un imbarco prioritario per le famiglie con bambini?" [Cheh oon eem-BAR-ko pree-o-ree-TA-ryo per ley fa-MEE-lyey kon bam-BEE-nee?]

ASKING FOR FLIGHT INFORMATION

1. "What time does the flight to Rome depart?" - "A che ora parte il volo per Roma?" [ah keh OH-rah PAR-teh eel VO-loh per RO-mah?]
2. "Is the flight delayed?" - "Il volo è in ritardo?" [eel VO-loh eh een ree-TAR-do?]
3. "Can you tell me the gate number for my flight?" - Puoi dirmi il numero del gate per il mio volo? [pwoi DEER-mee eel NOO-meh-ro del GATE per eel MEE-oh VO-loh?]
4. "Are there any available seats on the next flight?" - "Ci sono posti disponibili sul prossimo volo?" [chee SO-no PO-stee dee-spo-NEE-bee sool PROSS-ee-moh VO-loh?]
5. "What is the estimated arrival time in New York?" - "Qual è l'orario previsto di arrivo a New York?" [kwal eh lo-RAH-ree-oh pre-VEE-sto dee ar-REE-vo ah New York?]

6. "Is there Wi-Fi available on the plane?" - "C'è Wi-Fi disponibile sull'aereo?" [cheh Wi-Fi dee-spo-NEE-bee sool-lah-EH-reh-oh?]
7. "Can you confirm if my baggage will be checked through to my final destination?" - "Puoi confermare se il mio bagaglio sarà registrato fino alla mia destinazione finale?" [pwoi kon-fehr-MA-reh seh eel MEE-oh ba-gah-LYOH sah-RAH ree-jee-STRA-to FEE-no AHL-lah MEE-ah des-tee-NA-tsee-OH-neh fi-NA-leh?]
8. "Are there any restrictions on carrying liquids in hand luggage?" - "Ci sono restrizioni sul trasporto di liquidi nel bagaglio a mano?" [chee SO-no res-tree-ZYO-nee sool tras-POR-to dee lee-KWEE-dee nel ba-gah-LYOH ah MA-no?]
9. "Is there a connecting flight I need to be aware of?" - "C'è un volo di collegamento di cui devo essere consapevole?" [cheh oon VO-loh dee kohl-leh-ga-MEN-to dee DOO-ee DEH-vo eh-SSAY-reh kon-sa-peh-VO-leh?]
10. "Can I get a printed copy of my boarding pass?" - "Posso avere una copia stampata della mia carta d'imbarco?" [PO-sso a-VEH-reh OO-nah KO-pyah stam-PAH-tah DEH-lah MEE-ah CAR-ta deem-BAR-ko?]

PHRASES FOR DEALING WITH DELAYS OR CANCELLATIONS

1. "Excuse me, but my flight has been delayed. Can you provide more information?" - "Mi scusi, ma il mio volo è stato ritardato. Potrebbe darmi ulteriori informazioni?" [Mee SKOO-zee, ma eel MEE-oh VO-lo eh STAH-to ree-TAR-da-to. Po-TREB-beh DARR-mee oo-lee-TO-ree een-for-ma-tsee-OH-nee?]
2. "Is there an estimated time for the flight to be rescheduled?" - "C'è un orario stimato per la riprogrammazione del volo?"[Cheh oon o-RAH-ree-o stee-MA-to per la ree-proh-GRAHM-ma-tsee-OH-neh del VO-lo?]
3. "Are there any alternative flights available to my destination?" - "Ci sono voli alternativi disponibili per la mia destinazione?" [Chee SO-no VO-lee ahl-ter-NA-tee-vee dee-spo-NEE-bee per la MEE-a deh-stee-na-tsee-OH-neh?]
4. "Can I be rerouted on a different airline?" - "Posso essere indirizzato su una compagnia aerea diversa?" [POSS-so es-SEH-reh een-dee-RAHT-to soo OO-nah kom-PAN-ya ai-REH-ah DEE-ver-sa?]
5. "What are my options for compensation or rebooking?" - "Quali sono le mie opzioni per il risarcimento o la ri-prenotazione?" [KWAH-lee SO-no le MEE-eh op-TSEE-o-nee per eel ree-zar-chee-MEN-to o lah ree-pren-oh-ta-tsee-OH-neh?]
6. "Is there a customer service desk where I can get assistance?" - "C'è un banco servizi clienti dove posso ottenere assistenza?"[Cheh oon BAN-ko ser-VEE-tsee KLEE-en-tee DO-ve POSS-so ot-TEH-ne-reh as-SEES-TEN-tza?]

7. "Can I get a hotel voucher for the overnight delay?" - "Posso ottenere un voucher per l'hotel a causa del ritardo durante la notte?" [POSS-so ot-TEH-ne-reh oon VOW-tcher per LO-tel a kau-sa del ree-TAR-do door-an-teh la NOT-te?]
8. "Is there a designated area for stranded passengers to wait?" - "C'è un'area designata per i passeggeri bloccati in attesa?" [Cheh oon A-re-a dee-zee-GNA-ta per ee pahs-seh-JE-ree blok-KA-tee een a-TTEH-sa?]
9. "What are the procedures for rebooking or refunding the ticket?" - "Quali sono le procedure per la riprenotazione o il rimborso del biglietto?" [KWAH-lee SO-no le pro-CHE-du-re per la ree-pren-oh-ta-tsee-OH-neh o eel reem-BOR-so del bee-LYET-to?]
10. "Can I speak to a supervisor or manager regarding the situation?" - "Posso parlare con un supervisore o un responsabile riguardo alla situazione?" [POSS-so par-LAH-reh kon oon soo-per-vee-SO-reh o oon ree-spoN-sah-bee-leh ree-GWAR-do al-LAH see-too-A-tsee-OH-neh?]

DIALOGUES DURING THE FLIGHT

1. "Excuse me, could you please bring me a blanket?" - "Mi scusi, potrebbe per favore portarmi una coperta?" [Mee SKOO-zee, po-TREB-beh per fa-VO-re por-TAR-mee oo-na co-PER-ta?]
2. "May I have a pillow for more comfort?" - "Posso avere un cuscino per maggior comfort?" [POS-so a-VE-re oon koo-SEE-no per MAD-dyor COH-fort?]
3. "Is there any vegetarian meal option available?" - "C'è disponibile un'opzione di pasto vegetariano?" [Cheh dee-spo-NEE-beh oon-ohp-TSEE-o-neh dee PA-sto ve-ge-ta-REE-a-no?]
4. "Could I get a glass of water, please?" - "Potrei avere un bicchiere d'acqua, per favore?" [Po-TRAY a-VEH-re oon beek-KYEH-re DAH-kwa, per fa-VO-re?]
5. "Excuse me, but I seem to have dropped my pen. Can you help me find it?" - "Mi scusi, sembra che abbia perso la mia penna. Può aiutarmi a trovarla?" [Mee SKOO-zee, SEM-bra keh AB-bya PER-so la MEE-a PEN-na. PO-oh a-yoo-TAR-mee a tro-VAR-la?]
6. "Is there a charging port for electronic devices?" - "C'è una presa per la ricarica di dispositivi elettronici?" [Cheh OO-na PRE-za per la ree-ka-REE-ka dee dee-SPO-zee-tee e-let-tro-NEE-chee?]
7. "Excuse me, could you please lower the window shade?" - "Mi scusi, potrebbe per favore abbassare la tendina del finestrino? [Mee SKOO-zee, po-TREB-beh per fa-VO-re ab-bas-SA-re la ten-DEE-na del fi-nes-TREE-no?]
8. "Do you have any magazines or newspapers on board?" - "Ha qualche rivista o giornale a bordo?" [A KWA-lee ree-VEES-ta o jor-NA-leh a BOR-do?]
9. "Excuse me, may I use the restroom?" - "Mi scusi, posso usare il bagno?" [Mee SKOO-zee, POS-so oo-ZA-reel BA-nyo?]

10. "Is there a duty-free shop on the flight?" - "C'è un negozio duty-free sul volo?" [Cheh oon NE-go-tsee-o DOO-tee-FRAY soo VOL-o?]

REQUEST ASSISTANCE AT THE AIRPORT

1. "Excuse me, I need assistance with my luggage." - "Mi scusi, ho bisogno di assistenza con il mio bagaglio." [Mee SKOO-zee, oh bee-ZO-nyo dee as-see-STEN-tsa kon eel MEE-o ba-GA-lyo.]
2. "Could you help me find the baggage claim area?" - "Potrebbe aiutarmi a trovare l'area ritiro bagagli?" [Po-TREB-beh a-yoo-TAR-mee a tro-VA-re lar-EE-a ree-TEE-ro ba-GA-lyee?]
3. "Is there a wheelchair available for my companion?" - "C'è una sedia a rotelle disponibile per il mio accompagnatore?" [Cheh OO-na SEE-dee-a ro-TEL-le dee-SPO-nee-BEE-le per eel MEE-o ak-kom-pan-ya-TO-re?]
4. "Excuse me, could you direct me to the nearest information desk?" - "Mi scusi, potrebbe indicarmi l'ufficio informazioni più vicino?" [Mee SKOO-zee, po-TREB-beh een-dee-KAR-mee loof-fee-tcho een-for-ma-TSYO-nee pyoo vee-CHEE-no?]
5. "I've lost my boarding pass. What should I do?" - "Ho perso la mia carta d'imbarco. Cosa devo fare?" [Oh PER-so la MEE-a KAR-ta deem-BAR-ko. KO-za DEH-vo FA-re?]
6. "Is there a lost and found office at the airport?" - "C'è un ufficio oggetti smarriti all'aeroporto?" [Cheh oon oof-fee-tcho OBYET-tee sma-REET-tee al-LA-er-o-por-to?]
7. "Excuse me, I think I left my phone at the security checkpoint." - "Mi scusi, penso di aver lasciato il mio telefono al controllo di sicurezza." [Mee SKOO-zee, PEN-so dee a-VER las-see-A-to eel MEE-o te-LE-fo-no al kon-TROL-lo dee see-koo-RE-tsa.]
8. "Could you please inform me about the gate change?" - "Potrebbe per favore informarmi del cambio del gate?" [Po-TREB-beh per fa-VO-re een-for-MAR-mee del KAM-byo del GATE?]
9. "I'm feeling unwell. Is there a medical center or first aid station?" - "Mi sento male. C'è un centro medico o una postazione di primo soccorso?" [Mee SEN-to MA-le. Cheh oon CHEN-tro ME-dee-ko o OO-na po-sta-tsyo-NEE dee PREE-mo sok-KOR-so?]
10. "Excuse me, could you please call a taxi for me?" - "Mi scusi, potrebbe chiamare un taxi per me?" [Mee SKOO-zee, po-TREB-beh kee-a-MA-re oon TAK-see per me?]

22

OUTDOOR ACTIVITIES

Nature offers a sanctuary of beauty and tranquility, and Italy boasts an abundance of breathtaking landscapes to explore. Whether you're hiking through the majestic mountains, cycling along scenic trails, or enjoying water activities in pristine lakes and rivers, knowing the right phrases can enhance your outdoor adventure. In this chapter, we'll provide you with essential phrases for outdoor activities in Italy. From expressing your love for nature to seeking directions and engaging in conversations with fellow nature enthusiasts, you'll feel confident and prepared to immerse yourself in the splendor of Italy's natural wonders. Get ready to embark on an unforgettable tour in nature!

Feel free to adjust and personalize the introduction to fit your needs and writing style.

COMMON OUTDOOR WORDS

1. "Tree" - "Albero" - [ahl-BEH-roh]
2. "Flower" - "Fiore" - [FYOH-reh]

3. "Sun" - "Sole" - [SOH-leh]
4. "Mountain" - "Montagna" - [mon-TAH-nyah]
5. "River" - "Fiume" - [FYOO-meh]
6. "Lake" - "Lago" - [LAH-goh]
7. "Beach" - "Spiaggia" - [spyahj-jah]
8. "Forest" - "Foresta" - [foh-REH-stah]
9. "Waterfall" - "Cascata" - [kahs-KAH-tah]
10. "Rain" - "Pioggia" - [pee-OH-jah]
11. "Wind" - "Vento" - [VEN-toh]
12. "Bird" - "Uccello" - [ooh-CHEHL-loh]
13. "Butterfly" - "Farfalla" - [fahr-FAL-lah]
14. "Fish" - "Pesce" - [PEH-sheh]
15. "Star" - "Stella" - [STEL-lah]
16. "Forest" - "Bosco" - [BOHS-koh]
17. "Grass" - "Erba" - [EHR-bah]
18. "Sky" - "Cielo" - [CHEE-eh-loh]
19. "Island" - "Isola" - [EE-soh-lah]
20. "Wildlife" - "Fauna selvatica" - [FAH-oo-nah sehl-VEE-kah-tee-kah]
21. "Thunderstorm" - "Temporale" - [tem-po-RAH-leh]
22. "Bird" - "Uccello" - [oo-CHEHL-loh]
23. "Butterfly" - "Farfalla" - [far-FAHL-lah]
24. "Forest" - "Foresta" - [foh-REH-stah]
25. "River" - "Fiume" - [FYOO-meh]
26. "Island" - "Isola" - [ee-SOH-lah]
27. "Sunflower" - "Girasole" - [jee-rah-SOH-leh]
28. "Hiking" - "Escursionismo" - [es-koor-syoh-NEES-moh]
29. "Rainbow" - "Arcobaleno" - [ahr-koh-BAH-leh-noh]
30. "Volcano" - "Vulcano" - [vool-KAH-noh]
31. "Creek" - "Ruscello" - [roo-SHEHL-loh]
32. "Marsh" - "Palude" - [pah-LOO-deh]
33. "Pine tree" - "Pino" - [PEE-noh]
34. "Waterfall" - "Cascata" - [kah-SKAH-tah]
35. "Sunset" - "Tramonto" - [trah-MON-toh]
36. "Canyon" - "Canyon" - [KAH-nyon]
37. "Moss" - "Muschio" - [MOO-skyoh]
38. "Tropical" - "Tropicale" - [tro-pee-KAH-leh]
39. "National park" - "Parco nazionale" - [PAR-koh nah-tsyoh-NAH-leh]
40. "Beach" - "Spiaggia" - [spyahd-JAH]

VOCABULARY FOR HIKING AND CAMPING

1. "I love hiking in the mountains." - "Amo fare escursioni in montagna." [AH-moh FAH-reh es-kur-SYOH-nee in mon-TAHN-ya]
2. "Let's set up the tent." - "Montiamo la tenda." [mon-TYAH-moh la TEN-da]

3. "The trail is beautiful." - "Il sentiero è bellissimo." [eel sen-TYEH-roh eh bel-LEES-see-moh]
4. "We need a map for the hike." - "Abbiamo bisogno di una mappa per l'escursione." [ab-BYAH-moh bee-ZOH-nyoh dee OO-nah MAP-pah pehr l'es-kur-SYOH-neh]
5. "I enjoy camping under the stars." - "Mi piace campeggiare sotto le stelle." [mee PYAH-che kam-peg-GYAH-reh SOT-toh le STEL-leh]
6. "Don't forget to bring a sleeping bag." - "Non dimenticare di portare un sacco a pelo." [non dee-men-tee-KAH-reh dee por-TAH-reh oon SAK-ko a PEH-loh]
7. "The view from the summit is breathtaking." - "La vista dalla cima è mozzafiato." [la VEE-stah DAL-lah CHEE-ma eh motz-za-FYA-toh]
8. "We need to pack some food for the hike." - "Dobbiamo preparare del cibo per l'escursione." [dob-BYAH-moh preh-pah-RAH-reh del CHEE-bo pehr l'es-kur-SYOH-neh]
9. "Let's follow the trail markers." - "Seguiamo i segnavia." [seh-GWEE-ah-moh ee sehn-NA-vya]
10. "Camping near the lake sounds perfect." - "Campeggiare vicino al lago sembra perfetto." [kam-peg-GYAH-reh vee-CHEE-no al LAH-go SEM-bra per-FET-toh]

ASK ABOUT THE ROUTE OR DESTINATION

1. "Excuse me, can you give me directions to the nearest trailhead?" - "Mi scusi, può darmi indicazioni per il punto di partenza più vicino?" [mee SKOO-see, pwoh DAR-mee in-dee-ka-TSYO-nee per eel POON-toh dee par-TEN-za pyoo VEE-chee-no]
2. "Which way should we go to reach the summit?" - "Quale direzione dovremmo prendere per raggiungere la cima?" [KWAH-leh dee-reh-TSYO-neh doh-VREH-moh pren-DEH-reh per rah-JOON-geh-reh la CHEE-mah]
3. "Do you have a map of the hiking trails in this area?" - "Hai una mappa dei sentieri escursionistici in questa zona?" [eye OO-nah MAP-pah dei sen-TYEH-ree es-koo-zee-o-NIS-ti-chee in KWEH-stah ZOH-nah]
4. "What's the difficulty level of this hiking trail?" - "Qual è il livello di difficoltà di questo sentiero escursionistico?" [kwahl eh eel lee-VEHL-loh dee DEE-fee-kohl-tah dee KWEH-stoh sen-TYEH-roh es-koo-zee-o-NIS-ti-ko]
5. "Is there a specific landmark or sign to look out for along the way?" - "C'è un punto di riferimento o un cartello da cercare lungo il percorso?" [chay oon POON-toh dee ree-feh-REE-men-toh oh oon kar-TEL-loh dah cher-KAH-reh LOON-goh eel per-KOR-so]
6. "Can you recommend any scenic spots or viewpoints along the trail?" - "Puoi consigliare dei punti panoramici o dei belvedere lungo il sentiero?" [pwoy kon-see-LYAH-reh dei POO-nee pah-no-RAH-mee-chee oh dei bel-veh-DEH-reh LOON-goh eel sen-TYEH-roh]

7. "How long does it usually take to complete this hiking route?" - "Quanto tempo di solito ci vuole per completare questo percorso escursionistico?" [KWAN-toh TEM-po dee so-LEE-toh chee VWOL-eh per kom-PLEH-tah-reh KWEH-stoh per-KOR-so es-koo-zee-o-NIS-ti-ko]

8. "Are there any safety precautions we should be aware of on this trail?" - "Ci sono delle precauzioni di sicurezza di cui dovremmo essere consapevoli su questo sentiero?" [chee SO-no DEL-leh pre-kow-TSYO-nee dee see-koo-REHT-sah dee kwee doh-VREH-mo es-SEH-reh kon-sa-PEH-vo-lee soo KWEH-stoh sen-TYEH-roh]

9. "Is there a designated camping area near the hiking route?" - "C'è una zona camping designata vicino al sentiero escursionistico?" [chay OO-nah ZOH-nah KAM-ping dee-zee-GNAH-tah VEE-chee-noh ahl sen-TYEH-roh es-koo-zee-o-NIS-ti-ko]

10. "What are some other popular hiking destinations in this region?" - "Quali sono altre mete escursionistiche popolari in questa regione?" [KWAL-ee SO-no AL-tre MEH-te es-koo-zee-o-NIS-ti-che pop-o-LAH-ree in KWEH-stah reh-DJOH-neh]

PHRASES FOR BIRDWATCHING OR NATURE PHOTOGRAPHY

1. "Look, there's a beautiful bird perched on that tree!" - "Guarda, c'è un bellissimo uccello posato su quell'albero!" [gwar-DA, cheh oon bel-lee-SEE-moh oot-CHEL-loh po-SAH-toh soo kwell-AL-beh-ro]

2. "Do you know what species of bird that is?" - "Sai di che specie è quell'uccello?" [sahy dee keh speh-TSYEH eh kwell-oot-CHEL-lo]

3. "I spotted a rare bird. It's not commonly seen in this area." - "Ho avvistato un uccello raro. Non è comune vederlo in questa zona." [oh av-vee-STAH-toh oon oot-CHEL-loh RAH-roh. non eh co-MOO-neh ve-DEHR-loh in KWEH-stah ZOH-nah]

4. "Let's be quiet and observe the birds from a distance." - "Rimaniamo in silenzio e osserviamo gli uccelli da lontano." [ree-mah-NEE-ah-moh in see-LEN-tsyoh eh os-ser-VEE-ah-moh glee oot-CHEL-lee DAH lohn-TAH-noh]

5. "I brought my camera to capture the beauty of nature." - "Ho portato la mia fotocamera per catturare la bellezza della natura." [oh por-TAH-toh lah MEE-ah fo-toh-KAH-meh-rah per ka-too-RAH-reh lah bel-LET-tsa del-LAH nah-TOO-rah]

6. "Look at the colors of that bird's plumage. It's stunning!" - "Guarda i colori del piumaggio di quell'uccello. È stupefacente!" [gwar-DA ee ko-LOH-ree del pyoo-mah-JOH dee kwell-oot-CHEL-loh. eh stoo-peh-FAH-chehn-teh]

7. "The bird's call sounds so melodious." - "Il canto dell'uccello suona così melodioso." [eel KAHN-toh dell-oot-CHEL-loh soo-OH-nah KOH-zee meh-loh-DEE-oh-soh]

8. "Let's set up our binoculars for a better view of the birds." - "Prepariamo i nostri binocoli per una visione migliore degli uccelli." [preh-pah-REE-ah-moh ee NOH-stree bee-noh-KOH-lee per OO-nah vee-TSYOH-neh meel-YOH-reh day oot-CHEL-lee]

9. "Do you know any good spots for birdwatching around here?" - "Conosci dei buoni posti per l'osservazione degli uccelli in questa zona?" [koh-NOH-shee day BWOH-nee poh-STEE per loss-ehr-vah-TSYOH-neh day oot-CHEL-lee in KWEH-stah ZOH-nah]

10. "I'm amazed by the diversity of bird species in this habitat." - "Sono stupito dalla diversità di specie di uccelli in questo habitat." [SOH-noh stoo-PEE-toh DAH-lah dee-ver-SEE-tah dee SPEH-tsee dee oot-CHEL-lee in KWEH-sto ah-bee-TAHT]

INTERACTING WITH OTHER HIKERS

1. "Hello, are you enjoying the hike so far?" - "Ciao, stai apprezzando l'escursione finora?" [CHAO, stai ap-prez-ZAN-do l'es-kur-SIO-ne fi-NO-ra?]

2. "Do you know how much longer it takes to reach the summit?" - "Sai quanto tempo ci vuole ancora per raggiungere la vetta?" [SAI KWAN-to TEM-po chi VWO-le an-KO-ra per rag-GIUN-ge-re la VET-ta?]

3. "Let's take a short break and enjoy the breathtaking view." - "Facciamo una breve pausa e godiamoci la vista mozzafiato." [fa-CHIAMO oo-na BRE-ve PAU-sa e go-DIA-mo-chi la VI-sta mot-za-FYA-to.]

4. "Do you have any recommendations for scenic trails in this area?" - "Hai qualche consiglio su sentieri panoramici in questa zona?" [HAI QUAL-che con-SIL-yo soo sen-TYE-ri pa-no-RA-mee-chee in KWE-sta ZO-na?]

5. "I forgot to bring a map. Do you mind if I hike with you?" - "Ho dimenticato la mappa. Ti dispiace se faccio l'escursione con te?" [ho dee-men-TEE-ka-to la MAP-pa. Ti dees-PEE-a-che se FA-cho les-kur-SYO-ne kon te?]

6. "Watch out for slippery rocks along the trail." - "Attenzione alle rocce scivolose lungo il sentiero." [at-ten-TSYO-ne al-le ROK-ke skvo-LO-ze LOON-go il sen-TYEH-ro.]

7. "Are there any water sources nearby? I need to refill my water bottle." - "Ci sono fonti d'acqua vicine? Devo riempire la mia borraccia." [tchi SO-no FON-tee da-KWA vee-CI-ne? DE-vo ryem-PEE-re la MEE-a bor-RAT-cha.]

8. "Let's stick together for safety and companionship." - "Stiamo insieme per sicurezza e compagnia." [stya-MO een-SYE-me per see-KOO-RET-za e kom-PA-nya.]

9. "I've heard there's a beautiful waterfall further ahead. Have you seen it?" - "Ho sentito dire che c'è una bellissima cascata più avanti. L'hai vista?" [ho sen-TEE-to DEE-re ke tche OO-na be-LEE-see-ma ka-SKA-ta pyoo avan-tee. L'hai VIST-a?]

10. "Do you have any tips for camping in this area? This is my first time." - "Hai qualche suggerimento per il campeggio in questa zona? È la mia prima volta." [HAI QUAL-kwee soog-ge-ree-MEN-to per eel kam-PE-djo in KWE-sta ZO-na? Eh la MEE-a PREE-ma VOL-ta.]

MANAGING EMERGENCY SITUATIONS IN NATURE

1. "Hello, are you enjoying the hike so far?" - "Ciao, stai apprezzando l'escursione finora?" [CHAO, stai ap-PREZ-zan-do l'es-kur-SIO-ne fi-NO-ra?]
2. "Do you know how much longer it takes to reach the summit?" - "Sai quanto tempo ci vuole ancora per raggiungere la vetta?" [SAI QUAN-to TEM-po chi VWO-le an-CO-ra per rag-GIUN-ge-re la VET-ta?]
3. "Let's take a short break and enjoy the breathtaking view." - "Facciamo una breve pausa e godiamoci la vista mozzafiato." [fa-CHIAMO OO-na BRE-ve PAU-sa e go-DYA-mo-chi la VI-sta mot-za-FYA-to.]
4. "Do you have any recommendations for scenic trails in this area?" - "Hai qualche consiglio su sentieri panoramici in questa zona?" [HAI QUAL-che con-SIL-yo soo sen-TYE-ri pa-no-ra-MEE-ci in KWE-sta ZO-na?]
5. "I forgot to bring a map. Do you mind if I hike with you?" - "Ho dimenticato la mappa. Ti dispiace se faccio l'escursione con te?" [ho dee-men-TI-ca-to la MAP-pa. Ti dees-PEE-a-che se FA-ccio les-kur-SYO-ne con te?]
6. "Watch out for slippery rocks along the trail." - "Attenzione alle rocce scivolose lungo il sentiero." [at-ten-TSYO-ne AL-le ROC-che skvo-LO-se LOON-go il sen-TYE-ro.]
7. "Are there any water sources nearby? I need to refill my water bottle." - "Ci sono fonti d'acqua vicine? Devo riempire la mia borraccia." [tchi SO-no FON-tee da-KWA VEE-tchi-ne? DE-vo ryem-PEE-re la MEE-a bor-RAT-cha.]
8. "Let's stick together for safety and companionship." - "Stiamo insieme per sicurezza e compagnia." [stya-MO een-SYE-me per see-ku-RET-za e kom-PA-nya.]
9. "I've heard there's a beautiful waterfall further ahead. Have you seen it?" - "Ho sentito dire che c'è una bellissima cascata più avanti. L'hai vista?" [ho sen-TEE-to DEE-re ke tche EH OO-na be-LEE-see-ma ka-SKA-ta pyoo a-VAN-ti. L'hai VIST-a?]
10. "Do you have any tips for camping in this area? This is my first time." - "Hai qualche suggerimento per il campeggio in questa zona? È la mia prima volta." [HAI QUAL-kwee soo-ger-REE-men-to per eel kam-PEG-gyo in KWE-sta ZO-na? Eh la MEE-a PREE-ma VOL-ta.]

23

END OF YOUR TRIP

As your journey in Italy comes to a close, it's time to bid farewell and express your gratitude for the unforgettable experiences. This chapter, "Arrivederci Italia: Phrases for the end of the trip," provides you with the essential phrases to convey your appreciation, express your final thoughts, and leave a lasting impression. Whether you're saying goodbye to new friends, thanking locals for their hospitality, or expressing your love for this beautiful country, these phrases will help you navigate the emotional farewell. From heartfelt farewells to expressions of gratitude, this chapter equips you with the language you need to conclude your Italian adventure with grace and sincerity. Say goodbye in style and leave with cherished memories.

MOST COMMONLY USED WAYS IN ITALY TO GREET EACH OTHER

1. "Goodbye" - "Arrivederci" - [ar-ree-veh-DAYR-chee]
2. "Farewell" - "Addio" - [AD-dyoh]
3. "See you later" - "A presto" - [ah PREH-stoh]

4. "Until we meet again" - "Alla prossima" - [AL-lah PROS-see-mah]
5. "So long" - "Ciao" - [CHOW]
6. "Bye" - "Addio" - [AD-dyoh]
7. "Adios" - "Arrivederci" - [ah-ree-veh-DAYR-chee]

EXPRESSING GRATITUDE AND GREETINGS

1. "Thank you for the incredible hospitality during my stay." - "Grazie per l'incredibile ospitalità durante il mio soggiorno." [GRAH-tsee-eh per leen-KREH-dee-bi-leh oh-spee-tah-lee-TAH doo-RAHN-teh eel MEE-oh soh-JOHR-noh.]
2. "It was a pleasure getting to know you." - "È stato un piacere conoscerti." [EH STAH-toh oon pya-CHEH-reh koh-NOHS-ter-tee.]
3. "I'm grateful for all the unforgettable memories." - "Sono grato per tutti i ricordi indimenticabili." [SO-no GRA-toh per TOOT-tee ee ree-KOR-dee een-dee-men-tee-KAH-bee-lee.]
4. "Your kindness and generosity will always be remembered." - "La vostra gentilezza e generosità saranno sempre ricordate." [La VOH-stra jen-tee-LET-tsah eh jeh-neh-roh-ZEE-tah sah-RAHN-no SEM-preh ree-KOR-dah-teh.]
5. "I'm honored to have experienced the beauty of Italy." - "Mi sento onorato di aver vissuto la bellezza dell'Italia." [Mee SEHN-toh o-no-RAH-toh dee ah-VER VEESS-oo-toh la bel-LEH-tsa del-lee-TAH- lyah.]
6. "Grazie mille for the amazing memories." - "Grazie mille per i ricordi straordinari." [GRAH-tsee-eh MEE-leh per ee ree-KOR-dee stra-or-dee-NAH-ree.]
7. "Wishing you all the best." - "Vi auguro il meglio." [Vee ow-GOO-roh eel MEG-lyoh.]
8. "It's been a pleasure, and I hope to return one day." - "È stato un piacere, e spero di tornare un giorno." [EH STAH-toh oon pya-CHEH-reh, e SPEH-roh dee tor-NA-reh oon JOR-no.]
9. "Thank you for making my trip to Italy unforgettable." - "Grazie per aver reso il mio viaggio in Italia indimenticabile." [GRAH-tsee-eh per ah-VER REH-so eel MEE-oh VYAJ-jo een een-dee-men-tee-KAH-bee-leh.]
10. "Goodbye for now, but Italy will always hold a special place in my heart." - "Arrivederci per ora, ma l'Italia avrà sempre un posto speciale nel mio cuore." [AH-ree-veh-DEHR-chee per O-rah, ma lee-TAH-lyah AV-rah SEM-preh oon POH-sto speh-CHEE-ah-leh nel MEE-oh KWO-reh.]

PHRASES FOR HOTEL CHECK-OUT

1. "Good morning, I would like to check out of my room, please." - "Buongiorno, vorrei fare il check-out della mia camera, per favore." [BWOHN-johr-noh, voh-REH-ee FAH-reh eel chek-AWT dehl-lah MEE-ah KAH-meh-rah, pehr fah-VOH-reh.]

2. "Can you please prepare the final bill?" - "Può preparare il conto finale, per favore?" [POO-oh preh-pah-RAH-reh eel KON-toh fih-NAH-leh, pehr fah-VOH-reh?]

3. "I have enjoyed my stay here." - "Ho apprezzato il mio soggiorno qui." [oh ah-preht-TSAH-toh eel MEE-oh soh-JOHR-noh kwee.]

4. "Could you please arrange a taxi for me to the airport?" - "Potrebbe organizzare un taxi per l'aeroporto, per favore?" [poh-TREB-beh oh-gah-NAHR-reh oon TAHK-see pehr lah-eh-roh-PORT-toh, pehr fah-VOH-reh?]

5. "I would like to settle my bill and check out." - "Vorrei saldare il conto e fare il check-out." [voh-REH-ee sahl-DAH-reh eel KON-toh eh FAH-reh eel chek-AWT.]

6. "May I have a copy of the receipt, please?" - "Posso avere una copia della ricevuta, per favore?" [POH-soh ah-VEH-reh OO-nah KOH-pyah DEHL-lah ree-cheh-VOO-tah, pehr fah-VOH- reh?]

7. "Thank you for your hospitality during my stay." - "Grazie per l'ospitalità durante il mio soggiorno." [GRAH-tsee-eh pehr lohs-pee-TAH-lee-TAH DOO-rahn-teh eel MEE-oh soh-JOHR-noh.]

8. "Could you please arrange a wake-up call for tomorrow morning?" - "Potrebbe organizzare una sveglia per domattina, per favore?" [poh-TREB-beh oh-gah-NAHR-reh OO-nah SVAY-lyah pehr doh-MAHT-tee-nah, pehr fah-VOH-reh?]

9. "Is there anything else I need to take care of before checking out?" - "C'è qualcos'altro di cui devo occuparmi prima del check-out?" [cheh KWOHL-kohs-AHL-troh dee DOO-ee DEH-vo oh-koo-PAHR-mee PREE-mah del chek-AWT.]

10. "Goodbye and thank you for a wonderful stay." - "Arrivederci e grazie per un soggiorno meraviglioso." [ah-ree-veh-DEHR-chee eh GRAH-tsee-eh pehr oon soh-JOHR-noh meh-rah-vee-GYO-soh.]

DIALOGUES AT THE STATION OR AIRPORT

1. "Excuse me, could you please tell me where the train station is?" - "Scusate, potete dirmi dov'è la stazione dei treni?" [skoo-ZAH-teh, poh-TEH-teh DEER-mee doh-VEH lah stah-ZEE-oh-neh dey TREY-nee?]

2. "Is this the right platform for the train to Rome?" - "È questo il binario giusto per il treno per Roma?" [eh QWEH-sto eel bee-NAH-ree-oh GEE-oo-sto pehr eel TREY-no pehr RO-ma?]

3. "What time does the next bus to the city center depart?" - "A che ora parte il prossimo autobus per il centro città?" [ah keh OH-rah PAR-teh eel PROSS-ee-moh OW-toh-boos pehr eel CHEN-tro cheet-TAH?]

4. "Excuse me, is there a shuttle service to the airport?" - "Scusate, c'è un servizio navetta per l'aeroporto?" [skoo-ZAH-teh, cheh oon sehr-VEE-tsee-oh nah-VEHT-tah pehr lah-eh-roh-PORT-toh?]

5. "Can you please help me with the ticket machine?" - "Potete aiutarmi con la macchina del biglietto, per favore?" [poh-TEH-teh ah-yoo-TAHR-mee kohn lah MAHK-kee-nah del beel-LYET-toh, pehr fah-VOH-reh?]
6. "Excuse me, is this the line for the bus to the city center?" - "Scusate, è questa la fila per l'autobus per il centro città?" [skoo-ZAH-teh, eh QWES-ta lah FEE-lah pehr low-TO-boos pehr eel CHEN-tro cheet-TAH?]
7. "Can you tell me where I can find a taxi?" - "Potete dirmi dove posso trovare un taxi?" [poh-TEH-teh DEER-mee DOH-veh POHS-soh tro-VAH-reh oon TAH-kssee?]
8. "Excuse me, is there a left luggage service at the station?" - "Scusate, c'è un servizio di deposito bagagli alla stazione?" [skoo-ZAH-teh, cheh oon sehr-VEE-tsee-oh dee deh-poh-ZEE-toh bah-GAH-lee AHL-lah stah-ZEE-oh-neh?]
9. "Can you please direct me to the nearest taxi stand?" - "Potete indicarmi dove si trova il punto taxi più vicino?" [poh-TEH-teh een-dee-CAHR-mee DOH-veh see TROH-vah eel POON-toh TAH-kssee pyoo vee-CHEE-no?]
10. "Excuse me, is there a train to Milan departing soon?" - "Scusate, c'è un treno per Milano che parte presto?" [skoo-ZAH-teh, cheh oon TREY-no pehr Mee-LAH-no keh PAR-teh PREH-sto?]

ASK FOR INFORMATION FOR THE RETURN TRIP

1. "Can you please provide me with the schedule for the return trains?" - "Potete fornirmi l'orario dei treni di ritorno?" [poh-TEH-teh for-NEER-mee loh-RAH-ree-oh dei TREY-nee dee ree-TOHR-no?]
2. "Excuse me, are there any direct flights from Rome to my destination?" - "Scusate, ci sono voli diretti da Roma per la mia destinazione?" [skoo-ZAH-teh, chee SO-no VO-lee dee-REHT-tee da RO-ma per la MEE-a des-tee-na-tsee-OH-neh?]
3. "Can you help me find a reliable taxi company for the return journey?" - "Potete aiutarmi a trovare una compagnia di taxi affidabile per il viaggio di ritorno?" [poh-TEH-teh a-yoo-TAR-mee a tro-VAH-reh OO-na kohm-PAH-nee-a dee TA-ksi af-fee-DAH-bee-leh per il vee-AH-joh dee ree-TOHR-no?]
4. "Excuse me, where can I get information about the return bus schedule?" - "Scusate, dove posso trovare informazioni sull'orario dei bus di ritorno?" [skoo-ZAH-teh, DO-ve POS-so tro-VAH-reh een-for-ma-tsee-O-nee sul-lo-RAH-ree-O dei BUS dee ree-TOHR-no?]
5. "Can you tell me the departure gate for my return flight?" - "Potete dirmi il gate di partenza per il mio volo di ritorno?" [poh-TEH-teh DEER-mee eel GA-te di par-TEN-za per il MEE-o VO-lo dee ree-TOHR-no?]
6. "Excuse me, is there a direct train to my destination on the return journey?" - "Scusate, c'è un treno diretto per la mia destinazione nel viaggio di ritorno?" [skoo-ZAH-teh, cheh EH oon TREY-no dee-REHT-

to per la MEE-a des-tee-na-tsee-O-neh nel vee-AH-joh dee
ree-TOHR-no?]

7. "Can you provide me with the schedule for the return buses?" - "Potete
fornirmi l'orario dei bus di ritorno?" [poh-TEH-teh for-NEER-mee loh-
RAH-ree-O dei BUS dee ree-TOHR-no?]

8. "Excuse me, where can I find the information desk for the return
trip?" - "Scusate, dove posso trovare l'ufficio informazioni per il
viaggio di ritorno?" [skoo-ZAH-teh, DO-ve POS-so tro-VAH-reh loo-
FEE-tcho een-for-ma-tsee-O-nee per il vee-AH-joh dee
ree-TOHR-no?]

9. "Can you help me with the return ticket booking process?" - "Potete
aiutarmi con la prenotazione del biglietto di ritorno?" [poh-TEH-teh a-
yoo-TAR-mee kon la pre-no-ta-tsee-O-neh del beel-LYET-to dee
ree-TOHR-no?]

10. "Excuse me, is there a direct shuttle service to the airport for the return
journey?" - "Scusate, c'è un servizio navetta diretto per l'aeroporto nel
viaggio di ritorno?" [skoo-ZAH-teh, cheh EH oon sehr-VEE-tsee-O na-
VET-ta dee-REHT-to per la-eh-ro-PORT-to nel vee-AH-joh dee
ree-TOHR-no?]

REFLECTIONS ON TRAVEL: EXPRESSING OPINIONS AND FEELINGS

1. "Traveling to Italy was an incredible experience." - Viaggiare in Italia è
stata un'esperienza incredibile. [vee-AH-jah-reh een ee-TAH-lyah eh
STAH-tah oon-es-peh-ree-EHN-zah een-KREH-dee-bi-leh.]

2. "I'm so grateful for the opportunity to explore new places and immerse
myself in Italian culture." - Sono davvero grato per l'opportunità di
esplorare nuovi luoghi e immergermi nella cultura italiana. [SO-no
dahv-VEH-ro GRAH-toh pehr lo-por-too-NEE-tah dee es-ploh-RAH-
reh NOO-vee LOO-lee ee een-mer-JEHR-mee NEHL-lah kool-TOO-
rah ee-TAH-lee-AH- nah.]

3. "The beauty of Italy's landscapes left me in awe." - La bellezza dei
paesaggi italiani mi ha lasciato senza parole. [lah beh-LEHT-tsah dee
pah-eh-SAH-jee ee-tah-LYAH-nee mee ah lah-SYAH-toh SEHN-zah
PAH-roh-leh.]

4. "The warmth and hospitality of the Italian people made my trip even
more enjoyable." - La calda accoglienza del popolo italiano ha reso il mio
viaggio ancora più piacevole. [lah KAL-dah ak-ko-LYEN-tsah del po-
POH-lo ee-tah-LYAH-no ah REH-soh eel MEE-oh vee-AH-joh an-
KOH-rah pee-YAH-cheh-VOH- leh.]

5. "I will cherish the memories of this trip for a lifetime." - Conserverò i
ricordi di questo viaggio per tutta la vita. [kon-seh-VEH-roh ee ree-
KOR-dee dee KWEHS-to vee-AH-joh pehr TOOT-tah lah VEE-tah.]

6. "The rich history and art in Italy have left a lasting impression on me." -
La ricca storia e l'arte in Italia hanno lasciato un'impressione duratura su
di me. [lah REEK-kah STOH-ree-ah eh LAHR-teh een ee-TAH-lyah

AHN-no lah-SYAH-toh oon-eem-PREH-see-o-neh doo-RAH-stoo-rah soo dee meh.]

7. "I'm grateful for the chance to try authentic Italian cuisine." - Sono grato per l'opportunità di assaggiare la vera cucina italiana. [SO-no GRAH-toh pehr lo-por-too-NEE-tah dee as-sah-JAH-reh lah VE-rah koo-CHEE-nah ee-tah-LYAH-nah.]

8. "The vibrant and lively atmosphere in Italian cities is something I will always remember." - L'atmosfera vivace e vivace delle città italiane è qualcosa che ricorderò sempre. [lah-toh-smeh-RAH vee-VAH-cheh eh vee-VAH-cheh DEL-leh CHEET-tah ee-tah-LYAH-neh eh kwal-KOH-sah kee ree-KOHR-deh-roh SEM-preh.]

9. "Italy has captured my heart, and I can't wait to return one day." - L'Italia ha conquistato il mio cuore, e non vedo l'ora di tornare un giorno. [lee-TAH-lyah ah kon-kwee-STAH-toh eel MEE-oh KWOH-reh eh non VE-do LOH-rah dee tor-NAH-reh oon JOR-no.]

**TALK LIKE
A NATIVE!**

ITALIAN
SLANG

1

WHY YOU SHOULD KNOW SOME ITALIAN REGIONAL SLANGS

Italy has many different Italian dialects since the country is so large and has so many different cultural influences.

In this book, we will embark on a linguistic journey, exploring the colorful expressions, idioms, and dialects that make each region of Italy truly special.

From the rolling "r" of the Tuscan dialect to the melodic Neapolitan language, we will delve into the linguistic nuances that add flavor and depth to Italian communication.

Get ready to uncover the hidden gems of Italian regional slangs and enrich your understanding of Italian culture like never before.

LANGUAGE DIVERSITY IN ITALY

Italy is renowned for its remarkable language diversity, which is a reflection of its rich historical and cultural heritage. The country is home to numerous regional languages, dialects, and even micro-languages. Each region has its own distinct linguistic identity, showcasing a fascinating tapestry of linguistic variations. From the Romance languages spoken in the north, such as Lombard, Piedmontese, and Venetian, to the Sicilian and Neapolitan dialects in the south, the linguistic landscape of Italy is incredibly diverse. These languages and dialects not only highlight the local traditions and customs but also serve as a means of communication and identity for the communities that speak them. Exploring the linguistic diversity of Italy is a captivating journey through its rich cultural tapestry.

THE IMPORTANCE OF SLANG IN EVERYDAY COMMUNICATION

Slang plays a crucial role in everyday communication, serving as a vibrant and dynamic form of language expression. It adds color, depth, and authenticity to conversations, allowing individuals to connect on a more intimate level. Slang reflects the ever-evolving nature of language and captures the essence of contemporary culture. It is often used to create a sense of belonging and to establish social bonds within specific groups or communities. By understanding and using slang, one can navigate social interactions more effectively and connect with people on a deeper level. Slang also adds a touch of humor and informality, making conversations more lively and engaging. Embracing slang is an essential part of immersing oneself in the linguistic and cultural fabric of a community.

THE CHARACTERISTICS OF ITALIAN REGIONAL SLANGS

Italian regional slangs exhibit unique characteristics that reflect the diverse cultural and linguistic heritage of different regions. Each region has its own set of expressions, vocabulary, and pronunciation peculiarities that distinguish it from others. Regional slangs often incorporate local dialects, idiomatic expressions, and even foreign influences, resulting in a rich linguistic tapestry. These slangs not only serve as a means of communication but also reflect the distinct cultural identities and traditions of the regions. They contribute to a sense of regional pride and solidarity among locals, fostering a deeper connection to their roots. Exploring the characteristics of Italian regional slangs allows for a deeper understanding and appreciation of the linguistic diversity and cultural richness found throughout the country.

2

ITALIAN IDIOMS

To sound like a true Italian, there's nothing better than using idioms from time to time!

Here are for you the most commonly used idioms in Italy that you absolutely must know:

1. "In bocca al lupo" - "Into the mouth of the wolf." [een BOK-kah al LOO-po]: This is a way of wishing someone good luck.
2. "Costare un occhio della testa" - "To cost an arm and a leg." [kos-TAH-reh oon OK-kyoh DEL-lah TES-tah]: This means something is very expensive.
3. "Non avere peli sulla lingua" - "To not have hairs on the tongue." [non ah-VEH-reh PEH-lee SOOL-lah LEEN-gwah]: This means to speak one's mind, without holding back.
4. "Fare orecchie da mercante" - "To have ears like a merchant." [FAH-reh oh-REH-kee dah mer-KAN-teh]: This means to ignore something.

5. "Tirare il pacco" - "To throw the package." [tee-RAH-reh eel PAH-ko]: This means to stand someone up.

6. "Avere la botte piena e la moglie ubriaca" - "To have a full barrel and a drunk wife." [ah-VEH-reh lah BOT-teh PYEH-nah eh lah MOH-lyeh oo-BRYAH-kah]: This means to have your cake and eat it too.

7. "Avere le mani in pasta" - "To have one's hands in the dough." [ah-VEH-reh leh MAH-nee in PAS-tah]: This means to be involved in something, often in a slightly shady sense.

8. "Prendere lucciole per lanterne" - "To take fireflies for lanterns." [PREN-deh-reh loo-CHOH-leh per LAN-ter-neh]: This means to be fooled or deceived.

9. "Chi dorme non piglia pesci" - "Those who sleep don't catch fish." [kee DOR-meh non PEE-lyah PEH-shee]: This is an expression meaning the early bird gets the worm.

10. "Acqua in bocca!" - "Water in your mouth!" [AH-kwah in BOK-kah]: This means to keep a secret or to keep quiet.

11. "Far ridere i polli" - "To make the chickens laugh." [far ree-DEH-reh ee POH-lee]: This means something is so absurd or ridiculous, even the chickens would laugh.

12. "Essere al verde" - "To be at the green." [ES-seh-reh al VER-deh]: This means to be broke or to have no money.

13. "Non vedere l'ora" - "Can't see the time." [non veh-DEH-reh L'OH-rah]: This means to look forward to something.

14. "Avere un chiodo fisso" - "To have a fixed nail." [ah-VEH-reh oon KYOH-doh FEE-soh]: This means to be obsessed with something.

15. "Avere un cuore di pietra" - "To have a heart of stone." [ah-VEH-reh oon KWOH-reh dee PYEH-trah]: This means to be unfeeling or cruel.

16. "Stare con le mani in mano" - "To stand with hands in hands." [STAH-reh kon leh MAH-nee in MAH-noh]: This means to do nothing, usually when you should be doing something.

17. "Romper le scatole" - "To break the boxes." [ROM-per leh ska-TOH-leh]: This means to annoy someone.

18. "Cercare il pelo nell'uovo" - "To look for a hair in an egg." [cher-KAH-reh eel PEH-lo nell OO-oh-voh]: This means to nitpick or find unnecessary faults in something.

19. "Mettere il dito nella piaga" - "To put the finger in the wound." [meh-TEH-reh eel DEE-toh NEL-lah PYAH-gah]: This means to remind someone of a painful or sensitive issue.

20. "Piovere a catinelle" - "To rain buckets." [pyoh-VEH-reh ah kah-tee-NEL-leh]: This means it's raining very hard.

21. "Avere le mani bucate" - "To have holey hands." [ah-VEH-reh leh MAH-nee boo-KAH-teh]: This means to spend money frivolously.

22. "Dormire come un sasso" - "To sleep like a stone." [dor-MEE-reh KOH-meh oon SAH-soh]: This means to sleep very deeply.

23. "Essere nelle nuvole" - "To be in the clouds." [ES-seh-reh NEL-leh NOO-voh-leh]: This means to be daydreaming or not paying attention.

24. "Fare la gatta morta" - "To play the dead cat." [FAH-reh lah GAHT-tah MOR-tah]: This means to act coy or play hard to get.
25. "Non mi rompere i maroni" - "Don't break my chestnuts." [non mee rom-PEH-reh ee mah-ROH-nee]: This means don't annoy me or don't bother me.
26. "Cambiare discorso" - "To change the subject." [kam-BYAH-reh dee-SKOR-soh]: This means to divert the conversation to a different topic.
27. "Fare un buco nell'acqua" - "To make a hole in the water." [FAH-reh oon BOO-koh nel-LAH-kwah]: This means to waste one's efforts.
28. "Avere la testa tra le nuvole" - "To have the head in the clouds." [ah-VEH-reh lah TES-tah TRAH leh NOO-voh-leh]: This means to be absent-minded or to daydream.
29. "Tirare acqua al proprio mulino" - "To pull water to one's own mill." [tee-RAH-reh AH-kwah al pro-PRYOH moo-LEE-noh]: This means to act in self-interest.
30. "Fare il ponte" - "To make the bridge." [FAH-reh eel PON-teh]: This means to take an extended weekend by taking off the day between a holiday and the weekend.
31. "Avere un diavolo per capello" - "To have a devil for each hair." [ah-VEH-reh oon DYAH-voh-loh per ka-PEH-loh]: This means to be very angry.
32. "Essere in alto mare" - "To be in high sea." [ES-seh-reh in AHL-toh MAH-reh]: This means to be far from reaching one's goal.
33. "Sentirsi come un pesce fuor d'acqua" - "To feel like a fish out of water." [sen-TEER-see KOH-meh oon PEH-sheh fwohr DAH-kwah]: This means to feel uncomfortable or out of place.
34. "Mettere il carro davanti ai buoi" - "To put the cart before the oxen." [meh-TEH-reh eel KAH-roh dah-VAN-tee ah-ee BWOH-ee]: This means to do things in the wrong order.
35. "Tagliare la corda" - "To cut the rope" [tahl-YAH-reh lah KOHR-dah]: This means to run away or escape from a situation.
36. "Dare carta bianca" - To give a white card [DAH-reh KAHR-tah byahn-kah]: This means to give someone complete freedom to do what they want.
37. "Prendere due piccioni con una fava" - "To catch two pigeons with one bean" [PREHN-deh-reh DOO-eh pee-CHOH-nee kohn OO-nah FAH-vah]: This means to kill two birds with one stone.
38. "In un batter d'occhio" - "In a blink of an eye" [een oon BAHT-tehr dohk-kee-oh]: This means very quickly.
39. "Fare quattro chiacchiere" - "To make four chats" [FAH-reh KWAT-troh kee-AHK-kee-reh]: This means to make small talk.
40. "Avere l'acqua alla gola" - "To have water at one's throat" [ah-VEH-reh lah-KWAH AHL-lah GOH-lah]: This means to be in a difficult situation, similar to the English expression "to be in hot water".

3

NORTHERN ITALY: LOMBARDY, VENETO, PIEDMONT

Italian slang is not immune to the effects of globalization. As the world becomes more interconnected, cultural exchanges and influences have shaped the evolution of language, including slang. Globalization has introduced new concepts, trends, and expressions that have found their way into Italian slang, reflecting the impact of international cultures and the blending of linguistic influences. This chapter explores how globalization has influenced Italian slang, from the adoption of English words and phrases to the incorporation of slang from other languages. It delves into the dynamic nature of Italian slang, highlighting its ability to adapt and reflect the changing world we live in.

DISTINCTIVE FEATURES OF THE SLANG OF NORTHERN REGIONS

The slang of the northern regions of Italy is known for its distinctive features that set it apart from other dialects and slangs in the country. One notable character-istic is the influence of neighboring countries, such as France and Switzerland, which have shaped the language over time. This can be observed in the presence of

French loanwords and expressions in the slang of regions like Valle d'Aosta and Lombardy. Additionally, the northern slang often reflects the cultural diversity of the region, incorporating words and idioms from various local languages and dialects. This rich linguistic tapestry adds depth and uniqueness to the slang, making it a fascinating aspect of northern Italian culture.

EXPRESSIONS AND IDIOMS TYPICAL OF THE LOMBARD DIALECT

1. "A mandi in feragh" - "Let's go for a walk" - [a MAN-di in fe-RAH]
2. "Mi tira la brema" - "I feel homesick" - [mi TI-ra la BRE-ma]
3. "Fassa da piaser" - "Do as you please" - [FAS-sa da pia-SER]
4. "Cüra che la cüra l'è minga l'amüs" - "Take care, because care isn't funny" - [KÜ-ra che la KÜ-ra l'è MIN-ga l'a-MÜS]
5. "Sa dï se i l'è surt" - "Who knows if it's true" - [sa DÏ se i l'è SURT]
6. "Me ghe pens" - "I'll take care of it" - [meh gheh PENS]
7. "Vaghela" - "Wait" - [vah-GHEH-lah]
8. "Mangia bun" - "Eat well" - [MAHN-ja boon]
9. "Me dispias" - "I'm sorry" - [meh dee-SPYAHZ]
10. "Scusa mia" - "Excuse me" - [SKOO-zah MEE-ah]
11. "Vegn sciò" - "Come here" - [vehn SHOH]
12. "T'voeu ben" - "I love you" - [T'VOH-oo behn]
13. "Andeum via" - "Let's go away" - [ahn-DEH-oom VEE-ah]

VENETIAN SLANG: UNIQUE WORDS AND EXPRESSIONS

1. "No sta a magnar fegato" - "Don't fret"- [noh stah a MAH-nyar feh-GAH-toh]
2. "A tuto de culo" - "F**k you" - [a TOO-toh deh KOO-loh]
3. "Tirar via le scarpette" - "Take off like a rocket" - [TEE-rahr VEE-ah leh skar-PET-teh]
4. "A bota de l'acqua su'l fuoco" - "Put water on the fire" - [a BOH-ta deh LAH-kwah sool FWOH-ko]
5. "Gnente da invidiar ai salami" - "Nothing to envy from salami" - [NYEN-teh da een-vee-DYAR ahy sah-LAH-mee]
6. "A pròpio no ghe xe piazzo" - "There's simply no room" - [a PROH-pyo noh gheh zeh pyaht-tsoh]
7. "Dar de l'ombra" - "To annoy, bother" - [dar deh LOM-bra]
8. "A farsene du bali, xe parchè ghe xe deventà bisogno" - "To make a fuss, it's because there's a need" - [a far-SEH-neh doo BAH-lee, eh par-KAY gheh zeh deh-ven-TAH bee-ZOH- nyoh]
9. "Sarvargose de un gnaro e un quarto" - "To scatter like coins and a quarter" - [sar-var-GOH-seh deh oon NYAH-roh eh oon KWAR-toh]
10. "I fioi i fa i fioi, e i noni i fa i noni" - "Children act like children, and grandparents act like grandparents" - [ee FYOH-ee ee fah ee FYOH-ee, eh ee NOH-nee ee fah ee NOH-nee]

1. "Figata"-"Cool" - [fee-GAH-ta]
2. "Pirla" - "Idiot" - [PEER-la]
3. "Boh" -"I don't know" - [boh]
4. "Scialla" - "Take it easy, relax" - [SKYAH-lah]
5. "Sbatti" - "Effort, hard work" - [SBAT-tee]
6. "Ghigno" - "Ironic or mocking smile" - [GHEE-nyoh]
7. "Figo" - "Cool, fantastic" - [FEE-goh]
8. "Mara" - "Difficulty, problem" - [MAH-rah]
9. "Ramba" - "Attractive or sexy girl" - [RAHM-bah]
10. "Struscio" - "Stroll or walk around the city" - [STROO-shee-oh]

CENTRAL ITALY: TUSCANY, LAZIO, UMBRIA

REGIONAL SLANG IN HISTORICAL AND CULTURAL CONTEXT

Regional slang in Italy holds a significant place within the historical and cultural context of each region. These linguistic variations have deep roots in local traditions, dialects, and historical events, shaping the unique identity of each region. Understanding regional slang provides insights into the rich cultural heritage and diversity of Italy.

For example, the influence of historical occupations, such as maritime trade or agricultural activities, can be seen in the slang of coastal regions or rural areas. Slang terms related to specific local customs, traditional dishes, or cultural celebrations reflect the deep connection between language and cultural practices.

Moreover, regional slang reflects the social dynamics and interactions within local communities. It often serves as a marker of regional pride and identity, strengthening the sense of belonging among locals.

Exploring regional slang in its historical and cultural context unveils the fascinating layers of Italy's linguistic landscape, allowing visitors and language enthusiasts to delve deeper into the authentic essence of each region.

DISTINCTIVE FEATURES OF THE SLANG OF THE CENTRAL REGIONS

1. "Spassarsi" [spa-SAR-see] - It means "To have fun" or "To enjoy oneself" in Italian slang.
2. "Fà la piastra" [FA la PYAH-stra] - It means "To straighten one's hair" in Italian slang.
3. "Scialla" [SHYA-lah] - It means "Relax" or "Take it easy" in Italian slang.
4. "Cavolo" [KA-vo-lo] - It is used as a euphemism for "Cazzo," which means "Penis" in Italian. It is often used as an exclamation to express surprise, frustration, or emphasis.
5. "Magari" [ma-GA-ree] - It means "Maybe" or "I wish" in Italian slang. It is used to express a desire or hope for something.

TYPICAL EXPRESSIONS IN THE TUSCAN DIALECT

1. "Bischero" - "Silly" or "foolish" - [bi-SKE-ro]
2. "Ceccarelli" - "Sunglasses" - [che-CA-rel-li]
3. "Fiorentino doc" - "True Florentine" - [fio-ren-TI-no DOC]
4. "A far brutto!" - "To cause a mess!" - [A far BRUT-to]
5. "Non fare la gobbaccia!" - "Don't be snobbish!" - [NON fa-re la gob-BAC-cia]
6. "Darci una pippata" - "To have a casual conversation" - [dar-CHEE oo-na pip-PA-ta]
7. "Fà er cascamorto" - "To act like a playboy" - [FAH er cas-ca-MOR-to]
8. "Avere la panza piena de risate" - "To have a belly full of laughter" - [a-VEH-re la PAN-za pyeh-na de ri-SA-te]

ROMAN SLANG: COMMON WORDS AND IDIOMS

1. "Avere la faccia da carciofo" - "To have a disgruntled or irritated face" - [ah-VEH-reh lah FAH-chah dah kar-CHO-foh]
2. "Chi se fa li cazzi sua campa cent'anni" - "Those who mind their own business live a hundred years" - [kee seh fah lee KAHT-tsee SWAH KAHM-pah chehnt AHN-nee]
3. "Spaccare 'o culo a qualcuno" - "To break someone's backside" - [spah-KAH-reh oh KOO-loh ah kwal-KOO-noh]
4. "Mannaggia a 'zzoccola" - "Expression of frustration or anger" - [mahn-NAH-jah ah tsohk-KO-lah]
5. "Fà er matto co' li soldi" - "To act crazy with money" - [FAH er MAH-tto koh lee SOHL-dee]

6. "Tanto pe' cantà" - "Just for the sake of singing" - [TAHN-toh peh kahn-TAH]
7. "Fà er coccodrillo" - "To show false sadness or worry" - [FAH er kok-ko-DREE-loh]
8. "Fà er portoghese" - "To not understand anything" - [FAH er por-toh-GEH-zeh]
9. "Er mondo è bello perché è vario" - "Every person is different, and that makes the world interesting" - [ehr MOHN-doh eh BEHL-loh per-KAY eh VAH-ree-oh]

WORDS AND TERMS USED IN CENTRAL UMBRIA

1. "A' bona matina se vede l'amor" - "In the early morning, love can be seen." - [ah BOH-nah mah-TEE-nah seh VEH-deh lah-MOHR]
2. "Chi s'ariccorda, campa" - "Those who remember, live." - [kee sah-reek-KOR-dah, KAHM-pah]
3. "Cacio cacio maco maco" - "Small talk, empty words." - [KAH-cho KAH-cho MAH-ko MAH-ko]
4. "La panza nun fa er monaco" - "The belly doesn't make the monk." - [lah PAN-tsah noon fah er moh-NAH-koh]
5. "Nun mette lo pe' n'acqua" - "Don't put your foot in the water." - [noon MET-teh lo peh nah-KWAH]
6. "Er baccalà a tratti c'è" - "Codfish comes in waves." - [er bahk-kah-LAH ah TRAHT-tee cheh]
7. "A fagiolo d'argento, testa d'asino" - "A silver bean, donkey's head." - [ah fah-JOH-lo dar-JEN-toh, TEHS-tah dar-ZEE-no]
8. "Dare una sbruciacchiata" - "To take a quick look." - [DAH-reh OO-nah sbroo-chahk-KYAH-tah]
9. "Dormire come un ghiro" - "To sleep like a dormouse." - [dor-MEE-reh KOH-meh oon GEE-roh]
10. "Far la galletta" - "To make a fuss or complain." - [far lah gah-LEHT-tah]

5

SOUTHERN ITALY: CAMPANIA, PUGLIA, SICILY

Get ready to explore the colorful and lively world of slang in Southern Italy! In this chapter, we dive into the vibrant dialects and unique expressions of the regions of Campania, Puglia, and Sicily. From the enchanting Neapolitan dialect to the distinctive Pugliese slang and the expressive Sicilian dialect, you'll uncover a treasure trove of linguistic gems that reflect the rich cultural heritage of these areas. Immerse yourself in the local expressions, idioms, and colloquialisms that capture the essence of Southern Italian communication. Discover the warmth, passion, and authenticity of the people through their language, and enhance your cultural experience as you explore the dynamic slang of Southern Italy.

EXPRESSIONS AND IDIOMS TYPICAL OF THE NEAPOLITAN DIALECT

1. "Chiagne e fotte, fatto 'e mma'!" - "Cry and complain, but do it quietly!" - [KYAH-nyeh eh FOT-te, FAT-toh eh MA]

2. "A cuollo 'e cavallo, ciuccio 'e carrucola" - "With the neck of a horse, the head of a donkey" - [ah KWOL-loh eh ka-VAL-loh, CHOOK-choh eh ka-roo-KO-lah]
3. "Fà na pazzia 'e varca" - "To do something foolish" - [FAH nah PAHTS-see-ah eh VAR-kah]
4. "Chella è 'o core 'e Cacullo" - "That's the heart of Cacullo" (referring to someone who is stingy) - [KEL-lah eh oh KOH-reh eh ka-KOOL-loh]
5. "Dorme 'o lupo 'ncoppa 'o pecurillo" - "The wolf sleeps on the sheep" (referring to a dangerous situation) - [DOR-meh oh LOO-po in-KOP-pah oh peh-koo-REE-lloh]
6. "Mett'a scale 'o perdono" - "To put forgiveness on the stairs" (referring to forgiving but not forgetting) - [MET-tah SKAH-leh oh per-DOH-noh]
7. "Fà 'o napulitano" - "To act like a Neapolitan" (referring to being clever and resourceful) - [FAH oh nah-poo-lee-TAH-noh]
8. "E' 'na scarpa 'e cerasa" - "It's like a cherry shoe" (referring to something small and insignificant) - [EH nah SKAR-pah eh cheh-RAH-sah]
9. "Essere 'n'abbeveratoio" - "To be a watering hole" (referring to being the center of attention) - [es-SEH-reh nah-beh-veh-rah-TOH-ee-oh]
10. "Faje 'o vaso 'e notte" - "To do the night pot" (referring to doing something secretly or dishonestly) - [FAH-yeh oh VAH-soh eh NOT-teh]
11. "'O mare 'e capa 'e cafè" - "The sea is a head of coffee" (referring to a chaotic or confusing situation) - [oh MAH-reh eh KAH-pah eh ka-FEH]
12. "Piglià 'o moccio" - "To take the snot" (referring to taking advantage of someone) - [peel-YAH oh MOCK-koh]
13. "Fuje 'a vottola" - "To run like a top" (referring to running very fast) - [FOO-yeh ah voh-TOL-lah]
14. "Miette 'a prova" - "To put to the test" - [MYEH-teh ah PROH-vah]
15. "A panza ca' i ciuccio" - "The belly is full" (referring to being satisfied and content) - [ah PAN-zah kah ee CHOOCH-choh]
16. "A truove 'e vocce" - "To hear voices" (referring to being delirious or confused) - [ah TROO-oh-veh eh VOT-cheh]

These expressions and idioms typical of the Neapolitan dialect capture the unique cultural identity and linguistic richness of the region.

APULIAN SLANG: LOCAL WORDS AND EXPRESSIONS

1. "La iòsa" - "the noise" - [JO-sa]
2. "Zagn" - "bad dressed" - [ZA-gn]
3. "Je assà u dann" - "Resentment toward a person or situation" - [JE-ass-A'-u-d-ANN]
4. "Ce tip d gomm" - Literally, it means "rubber person", but it indicates a particular person - [KE-teep-d-Gomm]
5. "A sfazion" - "Certainly" - [A-sf-A-zio-N]
6. "Statt' bbun!" - "Bye" - [Sta-TT-BBun]

WORDS AND TERMS IN USE IN SICILY

1. "Mizzica" - This Sicilian term is used to express surprise, amazement, or admiration. It can be translated as "Wow!" or "Oh my!" - [meez-ZEE-kah]
2. "Mangiamu!" - This phrase is a common expression in Sicilian slang and it means "Let's eat!" It reflects the importance of food and the culinary culture in Sicily. - [mahn-JAH-moo]
3. "Pupi" - This word refers to the traditional Sicilian puppet theater. It is a popular form of entertainment and a unique cultural heritage in the region. - [POO-pee]
4. "Cumpari"- This term is used to address a close friend or buddy in Sicilian slang. It reflects the strong sense of camaraderie and friendship in Sicilian culture - [koom-PAH-ree]
5. "Sciù" - This Sicilian word is an affectionate term used to refer to a young girl or a little sister. It is often used in a playful and endearing manner - [SHOO]

THE INFLUENCE OF CULTURAL TRADITIONS ON REGIONAL SLANG

1. "Sagra"- This term refers to a traditional food festival or fair that celebrates a specific local product or dish. It reflects the influence of culinary traditions on regional slang. - [SAH-grah]
2. "Processione" - This word is used to describe a religious procession, which is an important cultural tradition in many regions of Italy. It demonstrates the impact of religious customs on regional slang. - [proh-ces-see-OH-neh]
3. "Ferragosto" - This term refers to the holiday of Ferragosto, which is celebrated on August 15th and marks the peak of the summer season in Italy. It showcases the influence of seasonal traditions on regional slang. - [fer-rah-GOH-stoh]
4. "Carnevale" - This word is used to describe the carnival season, which is celebrated with parades, costumes, and festivities in many regions of Italy. It highlights the impact of festive traditions on regional slang. [car-nay-VAH-leh]

6

ISLANDS: SARDINIA, SICILY, CAPRI ISLAND

Welcome to the fascinating world of island slang! In this chapter, we embark on a linguistic journey through the vibrant expressions and dialects of Sardinia, Sicily, and Capri Island. These islands have their own unique linguistic flavors that reflect their rich history and cultural diversity. From the melodic Sardinian dialect to the expressive Sicilian slang and the distinct dialect of Capri Island, you'll uncover a tapestry of words and phrases that transport you to the heart of island life. Immerse yourself in the local slang, uncover hidden idioms, and discover how language shapes the identity of these enchanting islands. Get ready to explore the linguistic treasures of Sardinia, Sicily, and Capri Island and enhance your understanding of the vibrant island cultures.

DISTINCTIVE FEATURES OF ITALIAN ISLAND SLANG

1. "Azzurro" - This word, meaning "blue" in English, is commonly used to describe the crystal-clear blue waters surrounding the islands. It reflects

the strong influence of the islands' natural surroundings on the local slang. - [aht-SOO-roh]

2. "Insulare" - This term refers to someone who is from or living on an island. It signifies a sense of identity and pride in being part of the island community, and it is a common slang term used to describe the locals. - [in-SOO-lah-reh]
3. "Cala" - This word is used to refer to a small cove or bay along the coastline. It reflects the importance of the islands' coastal landscapes and their connection to the local slang. - [KAH-lah]
4. "Pizzicato" - This term refers to a local traditional dance or music style often performed on the islands. It represents the cultural heritage and artistic expressions that have influenced the slang of these small communities. - [pee-tsee-KAH-toh]
5. "Insularità"- This word embodies the concept of island life and the unique characteristics and challenges that come with living on a small island. It is used in local slang to express the distinct lifestyle and sense of community found on these islands. - [in-soo-lah-REE-tah]

These examples illustrate how the geographical, cultural, and social aspects of small Italian islands shape their distinct slang. The natural environment, local traditions, and community dynamics all contribute to the unique vocabulary and expressions that are characteristic of these islands.

EXPRESSIONS AND IDIOMS TYPICAL OF THE SARDINIAN DIALECT

1. "Babbu mannu" - This expression literally translates to "big dad" and is used to refer to someone who is very influential or powerful in the community. It reflects the importance of family and hierarchy in Sardinian culture. - [BAH-boo MAH-noo]
2. "Sa chida" - This expression means "the thing" and is used to refer to something whose exact name you do not know or remember. It is an informal, colloquial way of referring to a specific object or situation. - [sa KEE-da]
3. "Issu est sa manna 'e su calzettu"- This idiom refers to a person who seems harmless or naive, but hides a cunning or mischievous side. The expression literally means "it's the sock hand," referring to a hidden part of an object that is not immediately visible. It is a way of describing someone who can surprise you with their cunning or cleverness. - [EESS-oo est sa MAN-na eh soo kal-ZET-too]
4. "Chi narat, gatat" - This Sardinian proverb means "he who speaks, errs." It is an invitation to think before speaking and to avoid saying things without thinking. It reflects the importance of thoughtfulness and wisdom in Sardinian culture. - [kee NAH-rat, GAH-tat]
5. "Sa babbu 'e su casu" - This expression translates to "the father of cheese" and is used to describe someone who is extremely generous or

hospitable. It reflects the importance of food and hospitality in Sardinian culture. - [sa BAH-boo eh soo KAH-soo]

SICILIAN SLANG: PECULIAR WORDS AND IDIOMS

1. "Fari lu cannistru" - This expression literally means "to be a cannister" and is used to refer to someone who does a lot of talking but no concrete action. It is a colloquial way of describing a person who talks a lot but does nothing concrete. - [FA-ree loo kan-nee-STROO]
2. "Custumari 'i sabbati" - This idiom refers to someone who has a habit of doing things only when it is too late or when circumstances require it. It refers to a person who always puts things off until the last moment. - [koo-stoo-MA-ree ee sa-BAH-tee]
3. "Nni rasciàri 'i curri" - This expression means "not letting go" and is used to refer to a person who holds a grudge or does not easily forget an offense or wrong suffered. It is a way of describing someone who holds resentment over time. - [nee ras-CHA-ree ee KOOR-ree]
4. "Ficcarìri 'nto vuttu" - This idiom refers to someone who minds their own business and does not meddle in the affairs of others. The expression literally means "to put one's face inside" and reflects an attitude of respect for others' privacy. - [fik-ka-REE-ree in-toh VOOT-too]
5. "Ncittàri comu 'n gattu 'nta sacca" - This idiom means "to stumble like a cat in a sack" and is used to describe an awkward or clumsy person. It refers to someone who has difficulty moving or coordinating. - [nchit-TA-ree KO-moo un GAT-too in-ta SAK-ka]

These examples represent some of the most distinctive words and idioms of the Sicilian dialect. They reflect the humor, creativity and vibrancy of Sicilian culture, offering a unique glimpse into the region's language and mentality.

WORDS AND TERMS IN USE ON THE ISLAND OF CAPRI

1. "Maruzzella"- This word is an affectionate term used to refer to a young and pretty girl on the Island of Capri. - [mah-roo-TSAY-lah]
2. "Pizzaiuolo" - This term refers to an expert pizza maker who prepares authentic Neapolitan pizzas on the island. - [pit-tsah-YOO-loh]
3. "Ammucciata" - This term refers to a moment of relaxation and seeking shade from the sun during a hot day on the island. - [ahm-moo-TCHA-tah]
4. "Scialuppa"- This word indicates a small traditional boat used for exploring the caves and coves around the island. - [shah-LOOP-pah]
5. "Caprese" - This term refers to something that is originated from or typical of the Island of Capri, such as Caprese salad, a dish made with tomatoes, buffalo mozzarella, and basil. - [ka-PREH-zeh]

These terms reflect the island's unique identity and culture, offering a special linguistic experience for those visiting this beautiful destination.

7

COASTAL REGIONS: LIGURIA, CALABRIA, MARCHE

1. Liguria: The coastal region of Liguria, home to cities like Genoa, has its own unique slang characterized by colorful expressions and local vocabulary influenced by the maritime culture and dialects of the area.
2. Calabria: Along the Calabrian coast, particularly in cities like Reggio Calabria, you can find a distinct slang that reflects the region's rich history and influences from Greek, Arabic, and Albanian languages, as well as local dialects.
3. Marche: The coastal region of Marche, known for its beautiful beaches, has its own slang that combines elements of the local dialect with influences from neighboring regions, resulting in a unique linguistic expression.
4. Coastal Influences: The coastal regions of Italy often have slang terms related to the sea, fishing, and beach culture. Coastal dialects may incorporate words and phrases specific to maritime activities and the coastal lifestyle.

5. Cultural Exchange: Due to their proximity to the sea, coastal regions have historically been centers of trade and cultural exchange. This has contributed to the development of unique slang words and expressions influenced by the interaction with different cultures and languages.

The slang characteristics of Italian coastal regions reflect the cultural, historical, and geographical aspects of these areas. They offer insights into the local identity and provide a fascinating glimpse into the linguistic diversity of Italy's coastal communities.

EXPRESSIONS AND IDIOMS TYPICAL OF LIGURIAN DIALECT

1. "Bella giüsta!" - Literally meaning "Just beautiful!" or "Perfect!" This expression is used to convey admiration or satisfaction with something. [Be-LA JYOO-sta]
2. "Sciò!" - This word is used to mean "come on" or "let's go" and is often used to encourage or motivate someone. [SHEE-oh]
3. "Fichissu!" - This expression is equivalent to "cool" or "awesome" in English. It is used to express excitement or admiration for something. [fee-KHEE-soo]
4. "Bogo bogo" - This phrase means "little by little" or "slowly but surely" and is often used to encourage patience or perseverance. [BO-go BO-go]
5. "Ciarì un bicciu" - This expression means "to have a chat" or "to talk a little." It is often used when inviting someone to have a conversation or catch up. [CHA-ree oon be-CHYOO]

These phrases add color and richness to the language and provide insight into the linguistic heritage of the region.

CALABRIAN SLANG: LOCAL WORDS AND IDIOMS

1. "Stu paisi è comu 'n funnu." - This town is like a labyrinth. [STOO pah-EE-see eh KOH-moo un FOON-noo]
2. "A muntagna l'è ricchi 'i frutti."- "The mountain is rich in fruits." [ah moon-TAHN-ya LEH REE-kee ee FROOT-tee]
3. "Cchiù 'nfurmazzioni cchiù s'ingurisicchia." - "The more information, the more confusion." [KYOO in-foor-maht-zee-oh-nee KYOO sin-goo-ree-see-KYAH]
4. "Vinni 'nta stu cuntrattu, scapà 'nta stu pittatù." - "Enter into this agreement, escape from this predicament." [VEEN-nee nta STOO kun-TRA-too, ska-PAH nta STOO pit-TAH-too]
5. "A matina u diavulu fà 'i surci." - In the morning, the devil makes his rounds." [AH ma-TEE-nah oo DYAH-voo-loo FAH ee SOOR-chee]

1. "Vernacolo" - Local dialect or regional language spoken in Marche. [vehr-NAH-koh-loh]
2. "Poggiolo" - Balcony or terrace typically found in traditional Marche houses. [poh-LYOH-loh]
3. "Burlamacca" - Noisy and lively celebration or procession often held during local festivals in Marche. [boor-lah-MAHK-kah]
4. "Brustico"- Traditional Marche dish made with roasted bread, garlic, olive oil, and various toppings. [broo-STEE-koh]
5. "Rosciola"- Very common olive variety in Italy, particularly in central regions such as Marche, Umbria, Abruzzo and Lazio. [ros-CHO-lah]

8

MOUNTAIN REGIONS: TRENTINO-ALTO ADIGE, VALLE D'AOSTA, ABRUZZO

Welcome to the picturesque mountain regions of Trentino-Alto Adige, Valle d'Aosta, and Abruzzo, where towering peaks and breathtaking landscapes shape the language and culture. In this chapter, we embark on a linguistic journey through the rich and diverse slang of these mountainous areas. From the distinctive dialects of Trentino-Alto Adige to the charming expressions of Valle d'Aosta and the authentic Abruzzese slang, you'll discover a world of words and phrases that reflect the unique mountain lifestyle. Immerse yourself in the local dialects, explore regional idioms, and embrace the cultural nuances that make these regions so special. Whether you're enjoying the alpine beauty of Trentino-Alto Adige, exploring the charm of Valle d'Aosta, or trekking through the rugged landscapes of Abruzzo, this chapter will guide you in mastering the mountain slang and connecting with the locals on a deeper level.

SLANG CHARACTERISTICS OF ITALIAN MOUNTAIN REGIONS

1. "Baita" - Refers to a mountain hut or cabin, typically used by shepherds or hikers. It is also used metaphorically to describe a cozy and rustic atmosphere. [bah-ee-tah]
2. "Rocciatore" - A term used to describe an experienced mountain climber or rock climber. It signifies someone who is skilled and knowledgeable in navigating mountainous terrain. [roh-chah-toh-reh]
3. "Risciò" - Refers to skiing in local dialects, particularly in mountainous regions. It represents the act of gliding down snowy slopes on skis. [rees-choh]
4. "Valanga" - Refers to an avalanche in Italian. It represents a significant natural event in mountainous regions and highlights the potential dangers associated with snowy slopes. [vah-lahn-gah]
5. "Rifugista" - A term referring to a person who is passionate about the mountains and a regular visitor to mountain lodges. It indicates someone who enjoys spending time in the mountains and appreciates the lifestyle and activities associated with them. [ree-foo-JEE-stah]

These additional phrases offer further examples of the slang characteristic of Italy's mountain regions, highlighting specific terms and expressions related to the life and culture of these areas.

EXPRESSIONS AND IDIOMS TYPICAL OF THE TRENTINO DIALECT

1. "Andar per marote" - This expression means "to wander aimlessly" or "to stroll around without a specific destination." It captures the idea of leisurely walking or exploring without a particular purpose in mind. [ahn-DAR per mah-RO-teh]
2. "Fàr una frola" - This phrase is used to describe someone who is daydreaming or lost in thought. It implies that the person is not fully present or engaged in the current situation. [FAR OO-na FRO-la]
3. "La fina del mèn" - Translated as "the end of the month," this expression is used to describe a challenging or difficult period, often referring to financial struggles that occur towards the end of the month when resources are running low. [LA FEE-na del MEN]
4. "Ghe n'ho le vûie in banca" - This phrase literally means "I have my desires in the bank." It is used to express a longing or a strong desire for something that is currently out of reach or unattainable. [GHE no le VOO-yeh in BAN-ka]
5. "Tener el nas de féndra" - This expression means "to be nosy" or "to have a curious nature." It refers to someone who is overly interested in other people's affairs and likes to gather information about them. [TEH-ner el NAHS de FEN-dra]

VALDOSTAN SLANG: REGIONAL WORDS AND IDIOMS

1. "Barna" - This word is used in Valdostan dialect to refer to a cabin or a small mountain shelter. It is often associated with the traditional stone and wood structures found in the Alpine region. [BAR-nah]
2. "Pistin" - This term is used to describe a narrow mountain trail or path, particularly one used for hiking or skiing. It is derived from the word "pista" (track) and is commonly used in the context of outdoor activities. [PIS-teen]
3. "Boué" - This expression is used as a friendly greeting in Valdostan dialect, similar to "hello" or "hi" in English. It reflects the warm and welcoming nature of the local community. [BOO-eh]
4. "Tsampa" - This word refers to a traditional Valdostan dish made from toasted barley flour. It is often used to make polenta-like dishes and is a staple food in the region. [TSAM-pah]
5. "Gabelou" - This term is used to refer to customs officers or border agents. In the Aosta Valley region, which borders France and Switzerland, border control has historically been an important part of daily life, and the term "gabelou" has become a colloquial synonym for such figures. [ga-be-LOO]

WORDS AND TERMS IN USE IN MOUNTAINOUS ABRUZZO.

1. "Scamitu"- This term refers to a narrow, steep path typical of the mountain trails of Abruzzo. These trails often have steep inclines and require some climbing skill. [ska-MEE-too]
2. "Majella" - This term refers to Majella, a mountain range in central Abruzzo. Majella is one of the region's main natural attractions and is known for its breathtaking views and rich biodiversity. [ma-JEL-la]
3. "Montepulciano" - This term refers both to a local grape variety that produces a famous red wine and to a town located on the slopes of Gran Sasso, the highest mountain in the Italian Apennines. Montepulciano d'Abruzzo is one of Abruzzo's most renowned wines. [mon-te-pool-CHEE-a-no]
4. "Pecora" - This term refers to the sheep, a common grazing animal in the mountainous areas of Abruzzo. Sheep farming and cheese production are traditions rooted in Abruzzo culture, and the sheep is a symbol of rural and pastoral life in the region. [pe-KO-ra]
5. "Rocche" - This term refers to the rocks or rocky outcrops found in the mountainous areas of Abruzzo. Rocks are often distinctive landmarks and offer spectacular views of the surrounding valleys. [ROK-keh]

1. "Quann 'u jurnu si chiammu su 'e muntagn" - When the day fades over the mountains. [KWAN oo JOOR-noo see KYAH-moo soo eh moon-TAHN-yah]
2. "A muntagna stè sempe pura" - The mountain is always pure. [ah moon-TAHN-yah steh SEM-peh POO-rah]
3. "Quann 'u ventu passa tra 'e cime" - When the wind passes through the peaks. [KWAN oo VEN-too PAH-sah TRAH eh CHEE-meh]
4. "A muntagna te cchiama" - The mountain calls you. [ah moon-TAHN-yah teh KYAH-mah]
5. "'U paesaggio 'e muntagn' sta a cchiù 'o parole" - The mountain landscape speaks louder than words. [oo pah-eh-SAH-jee-oh eh moon-TAHN-yah STAH ah KYOO oh pah-ROH-leh]

9

MINOR ISLANDS: PANTELLERIA, AEOLIAN ISLANDS, ELBA

Welcome to the enchanting world of the minor islands of Pantelleria, the Aeolian Islands, and Elba. Nestled in the sparkling waters of the Mediterranean, these islands have their own unique charm and linguistic flair. In this chapter, we delve into the intriguing slang spoken by the locals, uncovering the vibrant expressions and idioms that reflect the island way of life. From the volcanic landscapes of the Aeolian Islands to the rugged beauty of Pantelleria and the serene shores of Elba, you'll discover a rich tapestry of words and phrases that capture the essence of these captivating islands. Immerse yourself in the local dialects, learn the islanders' favorite sayings, and embrace the cultural nuances that make these places so special. Whether you're sunbathing on the beaches of Pantelleria, exploring the historic sites of the Aeolian Islands, or enjoying the laid-back atmosphere of Elba, this chapter will help you navigate the island slang and connect with the locals in a meaningful way.

SLANG CHARACTERISTICS OF SMALL ITALIAN ISLANDS

1. "'U mari e 'a jenti 'i l'isula se cunuscinu" - The sea and the people of the island know each other. [oo MAH-ree eh ah JEN-tee ee lee-SOO-lah seh koo-noo-SHEE-noo]
2. "'A jenti d''a picciridda" - The people of the little ones. [ah JEN-tee dah pee-chee-REE-dah]
3. "Quann 'u ventu s'abbassa sutta 'u mari"- When the wind calms down beneath the sea. [kwahn oo VEN-too sahb-BAS-sah SOOT-tah oo MAH-ree]
4. "'A vucca s'avvia a muntagna"- The mouth heads to the mountain. [ah VOOK-kah sahv-VEE-ah ah moon-TAHN-yah]
5. "'A lingua d''i isulani è d'oru" - The language of the islanders is golden. [ah LEEN-gwah dee ee-soo-LAH-nee eh DOH-roo]

EXPRESSIONS AND IDIOMS TYPICAL OF THE PANTELLERIA DIALECT

1. "'A Pantidderìa havi tanti scurpi"- Pantelleria has many surprises. [ah pan-tee-deh-REE-ah AH-vee TAN-tee SKOOR-pee]
2. "'O ventu chiàra e 'a manera calatina" - The clear wind and the Pantelleria way. [oh VEN-too kee-AH-rah eh ah mah-NEH-rah kah-lah-TEE-nah]
3. "'O sòle e 'a viticuzzità" - The sun and the vineyard. [oh SO-leh eh ah vee-tee-KOOT-see-TAH]
4. "'O mangianotte e 'e juornate caluruse" - The sleepless nights and the hot days. [oh man-jee-ah-NO-teh eh eh joo-or-NAH-teh kah-loo-ROO-seh]

WORDS AND TERMS IN USE ON ELBA ISLAND

1. "Mazzabòtte" - A large wooden tub used for grape stomping during wine production. [mahts-sah-BOT-teh]
2. "Babbaluccio" - A small edible snail commonly found on Elba Island. [bahb-bah-LOO-cho]
3. "Gariga" - A type of Mediterranean shrubland vegetation found on the island. [gah-REE-gah]
4. "Insùla" - The local dialect word for the island of Elba. [in-SOO-lah]
5. "Sciabica"- A traditional Elban fishing boat used for coastal fishing. [shah-BEE-kah]

THE PECULIARITY OF THE SLANG OF THE SMALLER ISLANDS

1. "Iscà" - A term used in the slang of smaller islands to mean "to go" or "to leave." [ee-SKAH]

2. "Ciurcì" - A local slang word meaning "to gossip" or "to chat." [choor-CHEE]
3. "Rombi"- Refers to the local fisherman dialect term for "fish." [ROHM-bee]
4. "Marechiaro" - A word used to describe the clear and calm sea, often associated with smaller islands. [mah-reh-kee-AH-roh]
5. "Pizzigallo" - A slang term used to describe a small fishing boat or dinghy commonly seen around the smaller islands. [pee-tsee-GAHL-loh]

10

FROM KITCHEN TO TABLE

Italy attaches great importance to cooking and food, so it is obvious that it has developed a number of sayings related to the cooking sphere.

Let's look at some of them together.

EXPRESSIONS AND IDIOMS RELATED TO FOOD AND COOKING

1. "L'appetito vien mangiando." - "Appetite comes while eating." This phrase means that the more you eat, the more you want to eat. [lapp-eh-TEE-toh vee-ehn man-jan-doh] -
2. "Far di necessità virtù." - "To make a virtue out of necessity." This phrase means to turn a difficult situation into an opportunity. [far dee neh-chess-ee-TAH veer-too]
3. "Chi mangia sano, vive sano."- "Those who eat healthy, live healthy." This phrase emphasizes the importance of a healthy diet for overall well-being. - [kee MAN-jah SAH-noh, VEE-veh SAH-noh]

4. "Mi piace la pasta al dente." - "I like pasta cooked al dente." This phrase expresses a preference for pasta that is cooked to a firm texture. [mee pee-AH-cheh lah PAH-stah al DEN-teh]
5. "Un caffè al volo, per favore." - "An espresso to go, please." This phrase is commonly used when ordering a quick coffee to be consumed immediately. [oon kaf-FEH al VO-loh, pehr fa-VO-reh]
6. "Mi raccomando, al dente." - "Please, al dente." This phrase is used to request pasta or rice cooked to a firm texture. [mee ra-com-MAHN-do, al DEN-teh]
7. "Portami un antipasto misto." - "Bring me a mixed appetizer." This phrase is used to order a variety of appetizers or starters. [por-TA-mee oon an-tee-PAS-toh MIS-toh]
8. "Mangia!" - "Eat!" This exclamation is commonly used in Italian households to invite everyone to begin eating or to encourage someone to eat more. [mahn-JAH]
9. "A tavola non si invecchia" - "At the table, one does not age." This saying underlines the value that Italians place on shared meals, seeing these moments not only as nourishment for the body but also for the soul. [AH ta-VO-lah non see in-VEHK-kee-ah]
10. "Prendiamoci una pausa caffè" - "Let's take a coffee break." This phrase highlights the significance of coffee in Italian culture, where taking a break to enjoy a cup of coffee is a cherished ritual. [pren-dee-AH-moh-chee OON-ah pah-OO-sah kah-FAY]
11. "Facciamo un aperitivo" - "Let's have an aperitif." Aperitivo is a pre-dinner drink and social gathering in Italian culture, often accompanied by small bites or snacks. [fah-chee-AH-moh oon ah-peh-ree-TEE-voh]
12. "Non si butta via niente" - "Nothing goes to waste." This saying reflects the frugality and resourcefulness of Italian food culture, where ingredients are often used in creative ways and leftovers are repurposed. [non see BOOT-tah VEE-ah NYEN-teh]

11

FASHION: TRENDS AND EXPRESSIONS

THE USE OF SLANG IN THE ITALIAN FASHION WORLD

1. "Che figo!" - "How cool!" This expression is commonly used in the Italian fashion world to express admiration or excitement about something stylish or trendy. [Keh FEE-goh]
2. "Sono alla moda" - "I'm fashionable." This phrase is used to indicate that someone is up-to-date with the latest fashion trends and styles. [SO-no ah-lah MOH-dah]
3. "Questo è uno stile unico" - "This is a unique style." It is often said to describe an outfit or a fashion piece that stands out and is distinctively original. [KWES-toh eh OO-no STEE-leh oo-NEE-ko]
4. "Ha uno stile impeccabile" - "He/she has impeccable style." This expression is used to compliment someone's sense of fashion and their ability to put together stylish and polished looks. [Ah OO-no STEE-leh im-peh-KAH-bleh]

5. "È di tendenza" - "It's trendy." This phrase is commonly used to describe something that is currently in fashion or popular in the fashion world. [Eh dee ten-DEN-tsa]

SLANG IN ITALIAN LIVING ROOMS AND CATWALKS

1. "Fare lo show" - "To put on a show." This phrase is used to describe a captivating and impressive performance, whether it's on a catwalk or in a living room setting. [FAH-reh loh SHOW]
2. "Essere sul pezzo" - "To be on top of things." This expression refers to being up-to-date and well-informed about the latest trends and developments, especially in the fashion industry. [ES-seh-reh sul PEH-tso]
3. "Avere stile" - "To have style." This phrase is used to describe someone who possesses a distinct and fashionable sense of personal style, whether it's in their clothing choices or interior design. [A-VEH-reh STEE-leh]
4. "Sgargiante" - "Flashy" or "loud." This term is often used to describe bold and attention-grabbing fashion choices or interior design elements that are vibrant and eye-catching. [s-gar-GIAN-teh]
5. "Passeggiata" - "Catwalk" or "promenade." This word is used to refer to a runway or catwalk, where models showcase the latest fashion designs during a fashion show. [pas-seg-GI-A-ta]

WORDS AND PHRASES IN VOGUE IN THE FASHION INDUSTRY

1. "Sprezzatura" - This term refers to effortless and natural elegance, a way of dressing that seems to be achieved without special care, but actually requires skill and style. [spret-tsah-TOO-rah]
2. "Prêt-à-porter" - This locution denotes ready-to-wear fashion, collections of clothing mass-produced and available for immediate purchase, differing from made-to-measure fashion. [pret-A-por-tay]
3. "Sartoria" - This word refers to a haute couture, fashion studio or fashion house that specializes in the creation of custom-made clothes of high quality and craftsmanship. [sar-toh-REE-ah]
4. "Sfilata" - This term denotes a fashion show, an event in which designers present their clothing collections on runways, showcasing the latest fashion trends and styles. [sfee-LA-tah]

12

SOCIAL SITUATIONS: PARTIES, MEETINGS, EVENTS

SLANG IN ROMANTIC ENCOUNTERS AND THE DATING WORLD

1. "I like this person, they're my type." - "Mi piace questa persona, è il mio tipo." - [mee pyah-cheh kwe-stah per-soh-nah, eh eel mee-oh tee-po]
2. "They made a strong impression on me at first sight." - "Mi ha fatto colpo a prima vista." - [mee ah fah-toh kohl-poh ah pree-mah vee-stah]
3. "We have good chemistry together." - "Abbiamo una bella chimica insieme." - [ab-bee-ah-moh oo-nah behl-lah kee-mee-ca een-see-em-eh]
4. "They make my heart beat faster." - "Mi fa battere il cuore più velocemente." - [mee fah baht-teh-reh eel kwore pyoo veh-lo-che-men-teh]
5. "There are butterflies in my stomach when we're together." - "Ci sono delle farfalle nello stomaco quando siamo insieme." - [chee so-no deh-leh far-fahl-leh neh-lo sto-mah-coh quan-doh see-ah-moh een-see-em-eh]

1. "No to discrimination!" - "No alla discriminazione!" - [noh ah-lah dee-skree-mee-nah-tsee-oh-neh]
2. "Freedom and equality for all!" - "Libertà e uguaglianza per tutti!" - [lee-ber-tah eh oo-gwah-lyahn-tsah pehr toot-tee]
3. "United we are stronger!" - "Uniti siamo più forti!" - [oo-nee-tee see-ah-moh pyoo fohr-tee]
4. "Human rights are fundamental rights!" - "Diritti umani sono diritti fondamentali!" - [dee-ree-tee oo-mah-nee so-no dee-ree-tee fon-dah-men-tah-lee]
5. "No to violence, yes to peace!" - "No alla violenza, sì alla pace!" - [noh ah-lah vee-oh-len-tsah, see ahl-lah pah-cheh]

3 SIMPLE STEPS TO ALWAYS CARRY THIS BOOK WITH YOU IN YOUR POCKET:

1) SCAN THIS QR WITH YOUR CAMERA

2) DOWNLOAD THE FREE PDF VERSION

3) READ IT FROM YOUR SMARTPHONE WHILE TRAVELING IN ITALY!

A FREE BOOK
FOR YOU!

✓ PUGLIA'S 5 MUST-VISIT LOCATIONS
✓ MORE THAN 50 AMAZING BEACHES
✓ A NATIVE'S ADVICE ON PUGLIA'S TASTIEST
✓ 200+ BEAUTIFUL FULL-COLOR PHOTOS TO HELP YOU
EASILY CHOOSE ACTIVITIES TO INCLUDE IN YOUR TRIP

SCAN THIS QR AND
DOWNLOAD NOW
YOUR FREE BONUS!

IMMERSE
YOURSELF IN THE
CULTURE!

ITALIAN TRADITION, ETIQUETTE AND CURIOSITY

1

INTRODUCTION

Few countries in the world can boast the number of traditions and customs that Italy boasts.

That's why it becomes essential to know the basic vocabulary for talking about traditions when you're about to travel to Italy, and in this book we'll look at them together.

Are you ready? Let's get started.

LEXICON OF TRADITION

1. "Tradition" - "Tradizione" - [trah-dee-TSYOH-neh]
2. "Custom" - "Usanza" - [oo-ZAHN-zah]
3. "Manners" - "Modi" - [MOH-dee]
4. "Etiquette" - "Etichetta" - [eh-tee-KET-tah]
5. "Culture" - "Cultura" - [kool-TOO-rah]
6. "Courtesy" - "Cortesia" - [kor-TEH-zyah]
7. "Festival" - "Festa" - [FEH-stah]
8. "Celebration" - "Celebrazione" - [cheh-leh-brah-TSYOH-neh]
9. "Ritual" - "Rituale" - [ree-TOO-ah-leh]
10. "Holiday" - "Vacanza" / "Festività" - [va-KAHN-tzah / feh-stee-VEE-tah]
11. "Greeting" - "Saluto" - [SAH-loo-toh]
12. "Respect" - "Rispetto" - [ree-SPEHT-toh]
13. "Polite" - "Educato" - [eh-doo-KAH-toh]
14. "Formal" - "Formale" - [for-MAH-leh]
15. "Informal" - "Informale" - [in-for-MAH-leh]
16. "Gift" - "Regalo" - [reh-GAH-loh]
17. "Dress code" - "Codice di abbigliamento" - [koh-DEE-chee dee ab-bee-lya-MEN-toh]

18. "Mealtime" - "Ora del pasto" - [OH-rah del PAH-stoh]
19. "Toast" - "Brindisi" - [brin-DEE-see]
20. "Taboo" - "Tabù" - [tah-BOO]

Did you know?

- In Italy, lunch is the most important meal of the day.
- It's customary to take a short nap after lunch, known as "riposino"[ree-po-SEE-noh]
- On Easter Monday, Italians often go on a picnic. This tradition is known as 'Pasquetta'[pah-SKET-tah].
- Aperitivo, a pre-dinner drink and snack, is a common tradition in Italy. [Ah-peh-ree-TEE-voh]
- Italians traditionally celebrate Christmas Eve with a feast of seafood, known as 'La Vigilia'. [Lah Vee-JEE-lyah]
- A common greeting in Italy is to kiss both cheeks.
- On New Year's Eve, Italians traditionally throw old items out of their windows to symbolize letting go of the past.

2

HISTORY AND CULTURAL ROOTS OF ITALY

1. "History" - "Storia" - [STOH-ryah]
2. "Culture" - "Cultura" - [kool-TOO-rah]
3. "Heritage" - "Patrimonio" - [pah-tree-MOH-nyoh]
4. "Ancestors" - "Antenati" - [ahn-teh-NAH-tee]
5. "Tradition" - "Tradizione" - [trah-dee-TSYOH-neh]
6. "Origin" - "Origine" - [oh-REE-jee-neh]
7. "Past" - "Passato" - [pahs-SAH-toh]
8. "Roots" - "Radici" - [RAH-dee-chee]
9. "Civilization" - "Civiltà" - [chee-veel-TAH]
10. "Monuments" - "Monumenti" - [moh-noo-MEN-tee]
11. "Archeology" - "Archeologia" - [ar-keh-OH-loh-jyah]
12. "Ancient" - "Antico" - [ahn-TEE-koh]
13. "Medieval" - "Medievale" - [meh-dee-eh-VAH-leh]
14. "Renaissance" - "Rinascimento" - [ree-nah-chee-MEN-toh]
15. "Modern" - "Moderno" - [moh-DEHR-noh]
16. "Contemporary" - "Contemporaneo" - [kohn-tehm-poh-RAH-neh-oh]

17. "Century" - "Secolo" - [SEH-koh-loh]
18. "Decade" - "Decennio" - [deh-CHEHN-nyoh]
19. "Era" - "Era" - [EH-rah]
20. "Epoch" - "Epoca" - [EH-poh-kah]

Did you know?

- Italian culture is heavily influenced by the Roman Empire and the Renaissance.
- The family is at the center of Italian social structure. [fah-MEEL-yah]
- Italian is the official language of Italy and is spoken by about 60 million people.
- Italy has 55 UNESCO World Heritage Sites, more than any other country in the world.
- Italy has a diverse culture because of its long history and geographical position in Europe.
- Many famous scientists and inventors, like Galileo Galilei and Leonardo da Vinci, were Italian.
- The Roman law and political system have had a profound influence on the democratic systems worldwide.

VALUES AND BELIEFS IN ITALIAN SOCIETY

1. "Values" - "Valori" - [VAH-loh-ree]
2. "Respect" - "Rispetto" - [ree-SPET-toh]
3. "Integrity" - "Integrità" - [een-teh-GREE-tah]
4. "Honesty" - "Onestà" - [oh-neh-STAH]
5. "Responsibility" - "Responsabilità" - [rehs-pohn-sah-bee-lee-TAH]
6. "Trust" - "Fiducia" - [fee-DOO-tyah]
7. "Loyalty" - "Lealtà" - [leh-al-TAH]
8. "Courage" - "Coraggio" - [koh-RAH-joh]
9. "Love" - "Amore" - [ah-MOH-reh]
10. "Patience" - "Pazienza" - [pah-TSYEN-tsah]
11. "Generosity" - "Generosità" - [jeh-neh-roh-SEE-tah]
12. "Gratitude" - "Gratitudine" - [gra-tee-TOO-dee-neh]
13. "Humility" - "Umiltà" - [oo-mee-LTAH]
14. "Compassion" - "Compassione" - [kohm-pahs-SYOH-neh]
15. "Freedom" - "Libertà" - [lee-BEHR-tah]
16. "Peace" - "Pace" - [PAH-cheh]

17. "Fairness" - "Equità" - [eh-KWEE-tah]
18. "Wisdom" - "Saggezza" - [SAJ-jeh-tsah]
19. "Kindness" - "Gentilezza" - [jen-tee-LEH-tsah]
20. "Dignity" - "Dignità" - [deen-GEE-tah]

Did you know?

- Italians value family greatly, considering it a central pillar of their lives.
- Friendship and loyalty are deeply respected values in Italian society."
- Italians believe in the importance of good food and sharing meals with loved ones.
- Respect for the elderly is a deep-rooted belief in Italy.
- Italians value 'bella figura', or making a good impression, especially in their personal appearance.
- Catholicism plays a significant role in Italian society and culture.

4

ITALIAN LITERATURE: FAMOUS WORKS AND WRITERS

1. "Writer" - "Scrittore" - [SKREE-toh-reh]
2. "Novelist" - "Romanziere" - [roh-MAN-tsyeh-reh]
3. "Poet" - "Poeta" - [poh-EH-tah]
4. "Playwright" - "Drammaturgo" - [dram-MAH-toor-goh]
5. "Biographer" - "Biografo" - [bee-oh-GRAH-foh]
6. "Essayist" - "Saggista" - [sahj-JEE-stah]
7. "Journalist" - "Giornalista" - [jor-nah-LEE-stah]
8. "Artist" - "Artista" - [ar-TEES-tah]
9. "Painter" - "Pittore" - [pee-TOH-reh]
10. "Sculptor" - "Scultore" - [SKOOL-toh-reh]
11. "Photographer" - "Fotografo" - [foh-TOH-grah-foh]
12. "Musician" - "Musicista" - [moo-ZEE-chee-stah]
13. "Composer" - "Compositore" - [kohm-poh-ZEE-toh-reh]
14. "Singer" - "Cantante" - [can-TAHN-teh]
15. "Actor" - "Attore" - [ah-TOH-reh]
16. "Dancer" - "Ballerino" - [bal-leh-REE-noh]

17. "Choreographer" - "Coreografo" - [ko-reh-oh-GRAH-foh]
18. "Designer" - "Designer" - [deh-ZINE-ehr]
19. "Architect" - "Architetto" - [ar-kee-TEHT-toh]
20. "Filmmaker" - "Cineasta" - [chee-neh-AH-stah]

Did you know?

- "Dante Alighieri, one of the most important Italian poets, was exiled from Florence and never returned."
- "Leonardo da Vinci was not just a painter, but also a scientist, engineer, and inventor."
- "Elena Ferrante, one of Italy's most successful contemporary authors, writes under a pseudonym and her true identity remains a mystery."
- "Caravaggio, known for his dramatic use of light and shadow in his paintings, led a tumultuous life and died under mysterious circumstances."
- "Italian playwright Dario Fo won the Nobel Prize for Literature in 1997."
- "The Divine Comedy by Dante is considered the greatest literary work composed in Italian and a masterpiece of world literature." - "Umberto Eco, famous for his novel 'The Name of the Rose', was also a renowned philosopher and semiotician."
- "Petrarch, another key figure in Italian literature, is often called the 'father of humanism'.
- "Italo Calvino was known for his fables and tales that mixed fantasy, history, and reality."
- "Michelangelo, the renowned Italian artist, was also a poet. His poetry often reflected his complex feelings about love and spirituality."

RELIGIOUS TRADITIONS AND RITES IN ITALY

1. "Easter" - "Pasqua" - [PAHS-kwah]
2. "Christmas" - "Natale" - [nah-TAH-leh]
3. "International Women's Day" - "Festa della Donna" - [FEHS-tah DEL-lah DOHN-nah]
4. "Carnival" - "Carnevale" - [car-neh-VAH-leh]
5. "Saint John's Night" - "Notte di San Giovanni" - [NOH-teh dee san joh-VAHN-nee]
6. "All Saints' Day" - "Ognissanti" - [oh-nyee-SAHN-tee]
7. "Procession of Mysteries" - "Processione dei Misteri" - [proh-chess-see-OH-neh dei mee-STEHR-ee]
8. "Race of the Candles" - "Corsa dei Ceri" - [KOHRS-ah dei CHEH-ree]
9. "The Palio" - "Il Palio" - [eel PAH-lyoh]
10. "Republic Day" - "Festa della Repubblica" - [FEHS-tah DEL-lah reh-POOB-lee-kah]
11. "Pentecost" - "Pentecoste" - [pen-teh-COH-steh]

12. "Assumption of Mary" - "Assunzione di Maria" - [ass-oon-TSYOH-neh dee mah-REE-ah]
13. "Feast of the Immaculate Conception" - "Immacolata Concezione" - [im-mah-coh-LAH-tah con-chep-TSYOH-neh]
14. "Saint Francis of Assisi" - "San Francesco d'Assisi" - [san fran-CHEHS-koh dass-EE-see]
15. "Saint Peter and Paul" - "San Pietro e Paolo" - [san pyeh-TROH eh PAH-oh-loh]
16. "Easter Monday" - "Pasquetta" - [pah-SKET-tah]
17. "Good Friday" - "Venerdì Santo" - [veh-nehr-DEE SAHN-toh]
18. "Epiphany" - "Epifania" - [eh-pee-FAH-nyah]
19. "Ash Wednesday" - "Mercoledì delle Ceneri" - [mehr-coh-LEH-dee delle CHEH-neh-ree]
20. "Feast of Corpus Christi" - "Festa del Corpus Domini" - [FEHS-tah del COR-pus doh-MEE-nee]

Did you know?

- On Easter Sunday, families gather for a special meal that often includes lamb and a traditional Easter bread called "colomba" [ko-LOM-bah].
- On Christmas Italian people set up of presepi [pre-SE-py] (Nativity scenes), celebrate the "Feast of the Seven Fishes" on Christmas Eve, and the arrival of "La Befana", a kind witch who brings gifts on Epiphany (January 6).
- On International Women's Day (March 8), it is customary to give women a sprig of yellow mimosa flowers as a sign of respect and appreciation.
- The Carnival period is marked by parades, masquerade balls, entertainment, music, and parties. The Venice Carnival is particularly famous for its elaborate masks.
- On the night of June 24, in celebration of Saint John the Baptist, bonfires are lit in many parts of Italy. In Florence, a historic soccer match in medieval costumes, "Il Calcio Storico", is also held.
- All Saints' Day is a public holiday in Italy on November 1. Italians pay their respects to the dead by visiting cemeteries and attending church services.
- During Holy Week in Trapani, Sicily, there is a 24-hour long procession featuring 20 floats of lifelike wooden sculptures depicting scenes from the Passion.
- The Corsa dei Ceri takes place in Gubbio, Umbria, in May. Three teams, each carrying a statue of a saint on a wooden octagonal prism (resembling a candle), race up the mountain.

- Palio di Siena is held twice a year, on July 2 and August 16, in Siena. Ten horses and riders, representing ten of the seventeen city wards, ride bareback around the Piazza del Campo.
- Republic Day is a national holiday on June 2, celebrating the day Italians voted to abolish the monarchy in 1946 and establish a republic. It is marked by military parades and political speeches.

SOCIAL ETIQUETTE AND HABITS

1. "Manners" - "Modi" - [MOH-dee]
2. "Tradition" - "Tradizione" - [trah-dee-TSYOH-neh]
3. "Custom" - "Costume" - [koh-STOO-meh]
4. "Habit" - "Abitudine" - [ah-bee-too-DEE-neh]
5. "Sociable" - "Socievole" - [soh-chee-eh-VOH-leh]
6. "Respect" - "Rispetto" - [ree-SPET-toh]
7. "Hospitality" - "Ospitalità" - [oh-spee-tah-lee-TAH]
8. "Courtesy" - "Cortesia" - [kor-teh-SEE-ah]
9. "Politeness" - "Educazione" - [eh-doo-kah-tsyoh-NEH]
10. "Punctuality" - "Puntualità" - [poon-too-ah-lee-TAH]
11. "Etiquette" - "Etichetta" - [eh-tee-KET-tah]
12. "Ritual" - "Rituale" - [ree-too-AH-leh]
13. "Gesture" - "Gesto" - [JEHS-toh]
14. "Celebration" - "Celebrazione" - [cheh-leb-ra-tsyoh-NEH]
15. "Conversation" - "Conversazione" - [kon-ver-sa-tsyoh-NEH]
16. "Gathering" - "Riunione" - [ree-oo-nee-OH-neh]

17. "Dinner" - "Cena" - [CHEH-nah]
18. "Aperitif" - "Aperitivo" - [ah-peh-ree-TEE-voh]
19. "Lunch" - "Pranzo" - [PRAHN-tsoh]
20. "Coffee" - "Caffè" - [kah-FEH]

Did you know?

- It is customary to wait until everyone is served before starting to eat.
- It is good manners to taste all the dishes present on the table.
- It's a common practice to use a piece of bread to mop up the remaining sauce on your plate. This is considered a compliment to the cook.
- When meeting friends and sometimes acquaintances, it's common to greet them with a kiss on both cheeks.
- Italians often drink their coffee standing at the bar, especially for the morning espresso.
- Before dinner, many Italians like to have an aperitivo - a drink and snack that serves as a social gathering to chat and relax before the meal.
- Sunday is traditionally a day for extended family to gather for a long, multi-course lunch.
- It is considered odd to order a cappuccino after 11 AM, especially after a meal, as Italians believe milk can hinder digestion.
- Italians are famous for using hand gestures while speaking, as it's an integral part of their communication.
- Being a little late (usually not more than 15-20 minutes) for social gatherings is common and not considered impolite. However, for professional appointments, punctuality is expected.

WEDDINGS AND CEREMONIES

1. "Wedding" - "Matrimonio" - [mah-tree-MOH-nee-oh]
2. "Bride" - "Sposa" - [SPOH-sah]
3. "Groom" - "Sposo" - [SPOH-soh]
4. "Bridesmaids" - "Dame d'onore" - [DAH-meh doh-NOH-reh]
5. "Best Man" - "Testimone dello sposo" - [teh-STEE-moh-neh DEHL-loh SPOH-soh]
6. "Priest" - "Prete" - [PREH-teh]
7. "Church" - "Chiesa" - [KYEH-zah]
8. "Reception" - "Ricevimento" - [ree-cheh-VEE-men-toh]
9. "Wedding Dress" - "Abito da sposa" - [AH-bee-toh dah SPOH-sah]
10. "Wedding Ring" - "Anello nuziale" - [ah-NEHL-loh noo-TSYAH-leh]
11. "Vows" - "Voti" - [VOH-tee]
12. "Toast" - "Brindisi" - [breen-DEE-see]
13. "Honeymoon" - "Luna di miele" - [LOO-nah dee MYEH-leh]
14. "Wedding Cake" - "Torta nuziale" - [TOHR-tah noo-TSYAH-leh]
15. "Invitations" - "Inviti" - [een-VEE-tee]

16. "Gifts" - "Regali" - [reh-GAH-lee]
17. "Flowers" - "Fiori" - [FYOH-ree]
18. "Bouquet" - "Bouquet" - [boh-KET]
19. "Wedding March" - "Marcia nuziale" - [MAR-chyah noo-TSYAH-leh]
20. "Guests" - "Invitati" - [een-vee-TAH-tee]

Did you know?

- The night before the wedding, the groom often organizes a serenade under the window of his bride. The groom usually arranges the serenade through a surprise appointment, and the bride is usually unaware of this until the serenade begins.
- At Italian weddings, "confetti" refers to sugar-coated almonds, that are typically given to guests as a wedding favor. They are usually packaged in groups of five, symbolizing health, wealth, happiness, fertility, and long life.
- Guests usually give cash as a gift at the wedding. They put money into a satin bag, called the "buste" [bus-THA], which the bride carries.
- A traditional Italian wedding dance is the "Tarantella", where guests hold hands and dance clockwise then counter-clockwise.
- Italian wedding receptions typically include a lot of dancing and singing. They are known for their lavishness, often including between four and six courses.
- In some regions of Italy, it is customary for the groom to have his tie cut into many tiny pieces that are then sold to the guests for cash.
- In traditional Italian weddings, it's not uncommon for friends and family to help prepare the food, making everything from scratch. This could range from the appetizers to the wedding cake.
- Italian weddings often start early in the morning and can go on until the early hours of the next day. Guests should be prepared for a long day of celebrating.

FUNERALS AND BEREAVEMENT

1. "Funeral" - "Funerale" - [foo-neh-RAH-leh]
2. "Coffin" - "Bara" - [BAH-rah]
3. "Cemetery" - "Cimitero" - [chee-mee-TEH-roh]
4. "Burial" - "Sepoltura" - [seh-pol-TOO-rah]
5. "Mourning" - "Lutto" - [LOOT-toh]
6. "Condolences" - "Condoglianze" - [kon-dohl-YAHN-tseh]
7. "Obituary" - "Necrologio" - [neh-kroh-LOH-joh]
8. "Wake" - "Veglia" - [VEH-lyah]
9. "Grief" - "Dolore" - [doh-LOH-reh]
10. "Tombstone" - "Lapide" - [LAH-pee-deh]
11. "Cremation" - "Cremazione" - [kre-ma-TSYOH-neh]
12. "Eulogy" - "Elogio funebre" - [eh-LOH-joh foo-NEH-breh]
13. "Funeral Home" - "Camera ardente" - [KAH-meh-rah ar-DEHN-teh]
14. "Hearse" - "Carro funebre" - [KAH-rroh foo-NEH-breh]
15. "Flowers" - "Fiori" - [FYOH-ree]
16. "Grave" - "Tomba" - [TOHM-bah]

17. "Requiem" - "Requiem" - [REH-kwee-em]
18. "Memory" - "Memoria" - [meh-MOH-ree-ah]
19. "Funeral Procession" - "Corteo funebre" - [kor-TEH-oh foo-NEH-breh]
20. "Will" - "Testamento" - [tes-tah-MEN-toh]

Did you know?

- In Italy, the mourning period can last for several months or even years. It's common for close family members to wear black clothes as a sign of mourning during this period.
- Most funerals in Italy are conducted in a Catholic church, where a Mass is held. The casket is typically open during the wake and the funeral, allowing mourners to pay their respects.
- Italian funerals are often large gatherings, attended by extended family members, friends, and even acquaintances.
- In small towns, it's still common to see funeral notices posted on walls or bulletin boards in public spaces, announcing the death and the funeral details.
- After the funeral, it is customary to have a meal, often in the deceased's home, where friends and family gather to share memories and comfort each other. This is often a time of community support and reassurance.
- Italians commemorate their loved ones on All Souls' Day (November 2) by visiting the cemetery, bringing flowers, and lighting candles at the gravesites of their departed loved ones.
- It's common for families to have a mausoleum or a shared family grave in Italian cemeteries. These can often be quite grand, showcasing beautiful stonework and intricate designs.
- Although cremation was not originally part of the Catholic tradition, it's becoming more common in Italy. However, burial is still the most common practice.

SPORTS IN ITALY

1. "Sport" - "Sport" - [spohrt]
2. "Team" - "Squadra" - [SKWAH-drah]
3. "Game" - "Partita" - [par-TEE-tah]
4. "Player" - "Giocatore" - [joh-ka-TOH-reh]
5. "Coach" - "Allenatore" - [ahl-leh-na-TOH-reh]
6. "Referee" - "Arbitro" - [ar-BEE-troh]
7. "Stadium" - "Stadio" - [STAHD-yoh]
8. "Score" - "Punteggio" - [poon-TEHD-joh]
9. "Goal" - "Gol" - [gohl]
10. "Championship" - "Campionato" - [kam-pee-oh-NAH-toh]
11. "Training" - "Allenamento" - [ahl-leh-na-MEN-toh]
12. "Tournament" - "Torneo" - [tohr-NEH-oh]
13. "Victory" - "Vittoria" - [veet-TOH-ree-ah]
14. "Defeat" - "Sconfitta" - [skohn-FEE-tah]
15. "Fans" - "Tifosi" - [tee-FOH-see]
16. "Penalty" - "Penalità" - [peh-nah-lee-TAH]

17. "Offside" - "Fuorigioco" - [foo-oh-ree-JOH-koh]
18. "Tactics" - "Tattiche" - [tah-TEE-keh]
19. "Fitness" - "Forma fisica" - [FOR-mah FEE-see-kah]
20. "Injury" - "Infortunio" - [een-for-TOO-nyoh]

Did you know?

- One of the oldest and most unique sports in Italy is Calcio Storico, a game that combines elements of soccer, rugby and wrestling. It is held annually in Florence, and its roots date back to the 16th century.
- Italy is famous for its passion for motorsport. Ferrari is one of the best known names in Formula 1, and motorcycling, particularly MotoGP, has great popularity.
- The Giro d'Italia is one of the most important bicycle races in the world, along with the Tour de France and the Vuelta a España. The first edition of the Giro was held in 1909.
- Serie A is one of the most watched and competitive soccer leagues in the world. Teams such as Juventus, AC Milan, Inter Milan and Napoli are known globally.
- Many minority sports have local popularity in Italy. For example, fencing is very popular, and Italy has a history of success in this sport. Others include archery and bocce.

TRADITIONS AND FOLK LEGENDS

1. "Traditions" - "Tradizioni" - [trah-dee-TSYOH-nee]
2. "Legends" - "Leggende" - [LEH-gen-deh]
3. "Tales" - "Racconti" - [rah-KOHN-tee]
4. "Myths" - "Miti" - [MEE-tee]
5. "Folklore" - "Folclore" - [fohl-KLOH-reh]
6. "Custom" - "Costume" - [koh-STOO-meh]
7. "Holidays" - "Festività" - [feh-stee-vee-TAH]
8. "Ceremonies" - "Cerimonie" - [che-ree-MOH-neh]
9. "Rituals" - "Riti" - [REE-tee]
10. "Celebrations" - "Festeggiamenti" - [feh-steh-jyah-MEN-tee]
11. "Festivals" - "Feste" - [FEH-steh]
12. "Stories" - "Storie" - [STOH-ree-eh]
13. "Beliefs" - "Credenze" - [kreh-DEN-tseh]
14. "Superstitions" - "Superstizioni" - [soo-per-stee-TSYOH-nee]
15. "Ancestors" - "Antenati" - [ahn-teh-NAH-tee]

16. "Heritage" - "Patrimonio" - [pah-tree-MOH-nyoh]
17. "Culture" - "Cultura" - [kool-TOO-rah]
18. "Customs" - "Usanze" - [oo-ZAHN-tseh]
19. "Folk tales" - "Fiabe popolari" - [FYAH-beh poh-poh-LAH-ree]
20. "Tradition bearers" - "Custodi delle tradizioni" - [koos-TOH-dee delle trah-dee-TSYOH-nee]

Did you know?

- The legend of the Befana tells of an old woman who brings gifts to children on the night of Epiphany, January 6. It is said that the Magi invited her to join them on their journey to see the baby Jesus, but she refused. Later, repentant, she tried to join them, but never found them. Since then, she has been leaving gifts for the children hoping that one of them will be Jesus.
- According to legend, Romulus and Remus were twins abandoned on the banks of the Tiber River and rescued by a she-wolf who suckled them. As adults, Romulus killed Remus in a quarrel and founded the city of Rome, naming it after himself.
- It is said that the Doge of Venice married the Adriatic Sea every year in a ceremony called "The Marriage of the Sea." This tradition symbolized Venice's dominance over the sea.
- This is not a legend in the traditional sense, but a series of unsolved murders that occurred between 1974 and 1985 around Florence, which contributed to many stories and conspiracy theories.
- According to legend, tarot cards were created in Bologna by a mystical philosopher. These decks of cards, used for divination, are still popular today.
- The legend tells of a master mason who could not complete the construction of the bridge. Desperate, he made a pact with the devil, promising the first soul to cross the bridge. The mason tricked the devil into letting a dog cross the bridge.
- Colapesce was a boy who loved to swim and could stay underwater for hours. According to legend, Colapesce dived into Mount Etna to support one of the columns that held up Sicily, and he has remained under the sea ever since.
- Azzurrina was an albino child who lived in a castle in Emilia-Romagna. During a snowstorm, she disappeared without a trace. It is said that every five years, on the longest day of the year, her voice can still be heard in the castle.
- Maurizio Gucci, the heir to the Gucci fashion empire, was murdered in 1995. His ex-wife, Patrizia Reggiani, was convicted of ordering the murder, in what has become one of Italy's most notorious crime cases.

- In the 1980s and 1990s, the Sicilian Mafia, known as Cosa Nostra, orchestrated a series of murders of magistrates, journalists, and politicians who opposed their power. Most famous among these are the assassinations of Judges Giovanni Falcone and Paolo Borsellino.

THANK

Hello Readers!!

Thank you from the bottom of my heart for choosing this phrasebook as your trusted companion during your Italian adventures.
It has been an absolute pleasure to be a part of your journey, and I sincerely hope that it has enhanced your experience in the most delightful ways, helping you speak like a real Italian when you travel among the beauty Italy has to offer!

If you don't know where to start for your trip to Italy, and you are looking for someone to help you plan your sightseeing itinerary, I suggest you visit my website myfriendpetru.com and contact me!
Finally, you should know that your satisfaction is of utmost importance to me, and I would be thrilled to hear about your thoughts and feedback on this book.

Your review will not only help me refine my content but also contribute to the growth of my book writing business, enabling me to continue providing valuable resources for travelers like yourself. Allow me to express my profound gratitude once more for choosing this phrasebook.

With heartfelt appreciation and friendship,
Francesco, your devoted Apulian friend.

FOLLOW ME
ON SOCIAL MEDIA

@petru.life

@petru.life

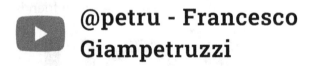

@petru - Francesco Giampetruzzi

Made in the USA
Middletown, DE
15 October 2023

40808720R00109